Shut'em Down: Black Women, Racism & Corporate America

Presented By
Dr. Carey Yazeed

Shero Books
Subsidiary of Shero Productions, LLC
Louisiana

Shero Books, a subsidiary of Shero Productions, LLC., P.O. Box 2405, Gonzales, LA 70707

Shut'em Down: Black Women, Racism and Corporate America

For information on booking co-authors for signings, interviews, and other events: www.shutemdownanthology.com or drcareyyazeed@gmail.com

ISBN: 978-0-9850316-4-0

Printed in the United States of America

Table of Contents

"The most disrespected person in America is the Black woman. The most unprotected person in America is the Black woman. The most neglected person in America is the Black woman."

~ Malcolm X.

Introduction

IN 2020 THE world was forced to stand still and witness the tragedy that is racism and how it has impacted people of color. With nothing to occupy our time as we waited for the COVID-19 pandemic to pass, citizens of the world slowly began to look at human life from a different perspective, or so we thought. This recognition that people with brown skin deserved the same dignity and humanity as everyone else was something many people had never really stopped to consider. Sure, we, as Black people, had created organizations like NAACP and Black Lives Matter, but history had shown us over and over again that our lives really didn't matter to some and unfortunately, many of us had suppressed that nonacceptance and silently moved in the background knowing that the American dream was just that, a dream.

Blacks had become numb to the brutality and harsh treatments we often fell upon, while other races simply turned their heads and acted as if everything was okay, when, in fact, it was not. But in the blink of an eye, we found ourselves watching the paradigm between race and humanity shift and the generational pain that Blacks had carried for centuries started to be heard and felt around the world. This time, no one could ignore us, or so we thought.

During that time, minorities began to speak out regarding the racial injustices, socioeconomic and health disparities that we had experienced at the hands of individuals and systems. Corporations were doing damage control, sending out emails to remind their clients and customers how much they supported Black lives, i.e. Black dollars, and how diversity and inclusion were integral parts of their companies. We drank the Kool Aid. We believed that people actually cared. The protective armor that many Blacks used to keep themselves from feeling the brunt of the blow life had dished out to them was being removed. The desensitization that we had built up to shield us from the impact of racism in our daily lives was slowly being tucked away.

In the past, Black women didn't talk about racism in corporate America. Instead, many of us suppressed the pain we felt from the humiliation we often endured. We forced ourselves to work harder to prove to our white superiors that we really were good enough. There were many days that I internalized and blamed myself for not reaching my career goals. I cried a lot and at one point took medication for anxiety and depression just so I could function at a dysfunctional job to support my family. Here I was with a whole Ph.D. barely making a living wage. I couldn't allow myself to speak the truth because I knew the consequences. I would never be smart enough. I would never be good enough. I would never blend into the whiteness of the American dream for which my parents and grandparents had hoped. Honestly, I became enraged when I looked at my white classmates from high school and those from graduate school and saw how unfair life really was. As racism suppressed my growth as a professional, it paved the way for my classmates to land the high paying jobs after graduation, buy the big home in the suburbs with a $10K gift from their parents as the down payment, and give their children a quality of life that my children and I would dream about for years. I had learned to navigate through the white space without being seen and trying my hardest not to piss anyone off as I did the best that I could with what I had.

It wasn't until the public outcry over the killing of George Floyd and the numerous Black souls that have been taken away from us way too soon by people who didn't look like us and could care less about us, that my emotions began to erupt like a volcano. I allowed myself to feel the ugly emotions I had neatly suppressed all of my professional life. It was also during this time that I began to notice I wasn't the only Black woman whose very existence was often devalued and had been mistreated by corporate America. As the outpour of hurt, pain and frustration took over social media, I began to hear stories that were similar to my own.

For once in my life, I realized that I wasn't alone and that myself along with other educated Black women were frustrated and tired. We didn't want to hear about the pay gap. We wanted someone to do something about it. We didn't want to take another class about diversity and inclusion, led by a white woman who didn't understand what it meant to be Black. We wanted to develop the curriculum and teach it ourselves. We didn't want to be overlooked for another job. We wanted our experience and education to speak for themselves and be provided the same opportunities as our white counterparts. We wanted access to the same business funds as Becky and Jane. We wanted to claim our piece of that American pie.

But just as the opportunity to speak and be heard had been given to us, it was quickly snatched away. Laws were passed to prosecute us as felons if we organized and participated in protests. Those diversity emails were replaced with ones that warned us to watch what we said on social media and to make sure it was in alignment with the mission of our various employers. At that moment in time, when God made the world stand still, what I hoped would have been progress, became the dream deferred Langston Hughes wrote about in his poem, Harlem. "Does it dry up like a raisin in the sun? Or fester like a sore–and then run?"

I realized that although the degrees are nice and look great on my resume and home office walls, there will always be a gap in pay between my white counterparts and myself. For once I finally understood that no matter how hard I try, life would never be as easy as my parents had dreamed for their young children or that Martin Luther King, Jr. preached about during the March on Washington.

The stillness has stopped. Some believe that us mattering for that brief moment in time is gone. But what hasn't been stifled are the voices of Black women. As we wean white America from our breasts and stop coddling a country that doesn't give a damn about us, we will no longer be ignored. Regardless if you like it or not, we have become stronger during this time and we are prepared to fight the ugliness called racism in corporate America and call out those who hate us because of the color of our skin and the curve of our hip. This ugliness may be woven throughout the fabric that many think makes America great, but we're here to shut 'em down!

Dr. Carey Yazeed

A Word From The Experts

The Trauma of Racism

Tiffany M Jenkins, LPC, LCADC, CCS

ON A DAILY basis, African Americans shoulder the trauma of living in oppression. At times, this oppression presents itself in more obvious ways like police brutality, but there are other times that the oppression is barely visible and much harder to explain. In these times, the oppression takes the form of microaggressions and faulty stereotypes that prevent women from showing emotion for fear of being labeled as "angry." This gaslighting, over time, can cause significant emotional wear and tear on the mind and body so much that psychologists have coined the term "racialized trauma" to accurately depict this situation. Racialized trauma shares the diagnostic criteria for post-traumatic stress disorder with one important distinction – the trauma experienced is solely because of the person's race.

A person who has experienced racialized trauma may exhibit many symptoms that are related to post traumatic stress disorder including:

- Distress related to the traumatic event. This distress can range from a mild discomfort to severe emotional outbursts.

Some individuals have flashbacks and nightmares that cause them to relive the event over and over long after the initiating event has passed. Reliving the event can cause distractions and interruptions that impede productivity and focus.

- Avoidance behaviors. Because of the pervasive nature of racism and discrimination, an individual who has experienced racism in the workplace may avoid going to work or interacting with certain individuals. This can have a significant negative impact on their work performance leading to other negative consequences.

- Intense anxiety or depression related to the traumatic experience. These changes in mood can occur all of a sudden or gradually over time. For some, the changes in mood are clearly related to the event while for others, the feelings can be turned inward and result in self-harming behaviors.

- Negative thoughts and feelings of distrust. When someone has experienced racism in the workplace, there is a sense that others witnessed the behavior but did nothing to intervene. This can result in a loss of trust in the organization, leadership, and fellow employees.

- Hypervigilance. Individuals who have lived through traumatic experiences develop a heightened startle response. They are more sensitive to their surroundings and are easily startled. In a work setting, this may mean that their increased sensitivity to discrimination makes them more likely to find issues even when there are none. Unfortunately, this can severely damage the work relationship with other team members causing further isolation and re-traumatization.

In addition to these symptoms, individuals who are regularly exposed to the mental strain of racism and discrimination are likely to develop significant mental and physical health issues including anxiety, depression, and heart disease. The good news is that there are tools and treatments available that can assist with decreasing the effects of racialized trauma which can help us to live our best lives.

- <u>Find a trauma-informed therapist and begin to process the events in a safe space.</u> If you can identify with any of the symptoms listed above, you need to talk to a licensed professional to work through your trauma. Therapy helps to resolve the negative feelings and emotions, release repressed feelings, and teaches new, healthy coping skills. Sites like therapyforblackgirls.com and therapyforblackmen.org are excellent resources to connect with Black therapists (yes, we do exist!).
- <u>Get involved!</u> Identify community organizations that help to empower individuals with the same experiences that you've had. Make a commitment to be the advocate for others that you wish you'd had.
- <u>Get active!</u> Finding a consistent exercise routine can help to stave off the negative mental and physical effects of trauma. Taking a brisk walk for 20-30 minutes a day can be helpful in fighting off heart disease and boosting your mood. Consult your physician to determine the workout routine that works for you.

Many African Americans have had at least one racially traumatizing experience in their lifetime, but too often we remain silent about it. We have to speak up, share our stories, and shed light on these issues so that we can bring healing and hope to ourselves and our community. *Remember, what happened may not be your fault but healing most certainly is your responsibility.*

Tiffany M. Jenkins is the founder of Awakening Change Counseling Services LLC located in Cherry Hill, New Jersey. As a licensed therapist, Tiffany's work centers around individuals struggling with anxiety, depression, and/or substance use. When not in the therapist's seat, Tiffany enjoys working with supervisors and managers to improve leadership outcomes through her innovative coaching curriculum. Awakening Change is also an accredited continuing education provider and Tiffany enjoys creating workshops and training programs to help clinicians to develop their skills.

Departure: We Don't Get Angry, We Get Equal

....

Monica Valentine, Ph.D.

THE TENSION IN the room was rising quickly and there was nowhere for me to escape. I was cornered, a Black woman, behind my desk. My boss, a white woman, was impatiently pacing back and forth in front of my office door waiting for me to change my mind about an offer she had just made. A coworker had retired a month prior from a more senior level, high-profile position. My boss had proposed that I accept the position as a lateral move with no additional pay. It was not so much what she said as to *how* she said it. There was no need to think about it, I turned the position down.

The Backstory.

All of the other employees in the department were white. They had higher salaries and less education than me: some didn't even have a college degree at all. Many of my colleagues were a visible part of the systemic "good 'ole boy" network hired by family friends and placed in entry level positions straight out of high school. They were eventually promoted up the ranks based on time in service, and notably, the color of their skin. I also started in an entry level position, but I did not enjoy the same social connections and white privilege to pad my career path.

Conversely, I advanced through personal grit, perseverance, strategy, and a white coworker who mentored and advocated for me until she retired.

Let's call the recent retiree, Sharon. Sharon was my *ally*. About a year before she retired, Sharon gave me a heads up that she would be leaving in a few months. Her point in confiding in me was so she could prepare me to take on some of her responsibilities in the event that our boss handed off her work to me as "other duties assigned," I would be prepared. She also looked me in the eye like a concerned grandmother and asked me if I knew why I was really hired. Caught off guard, I told her that I didn't know what she meant. Sharon got up from her desk and stuck her head out of the office door to look down the hallway to make sure no one was within hearing range. Then, she whispered, "I can't tell you now, but one day, there is something that I need to tell you about the initiative behind why she was forced to hire someone like you." That day never came, but truth be told, I already understood the meaning behind her words. Sharon showed me as much as she could over the next few months as well as after she retired, but I could never shake what she told me that day.

My boss was *forced to hire someone like me*. What my trusted friend meant was that my boss was forced to hire someone Black. All anyone had to do was just look around to see that our affirmative action numbers were terrible, but could it really be true that I was just a statistic? I knew that I was qualified for the position. I had the education. I had done my share of successful human resources consulting work, however, I had not worked for a corporation until that opportunity. All of this time, I had been so proud of my work and how well I had handled my position, as well as the additional roles that my boss kept giving me with no additional pay. I thought that being a team player and accepting extra work on the ladder of hope for advancement just came with the territory. I naively thought that if I proved myself, like anybody else, it would all pay off one day. Decoding the fact that *someone like me* meant *someone Black,* opened my eyes. I was just a token to this boss and to this company. It took me a minute to reconcile this hard, hurtful truth and realize I might need to plan both a path forward, and if necessary, an exit strategy.

I was giving this company my all, yet I was working twice as hard as my white counterparts. I didn't want anyone thinking that I wasn't pulling my own weight. I took on more tasks and found myself working through my breaks. My hard work was noticed alright. Leadership above my boss's pay grade began to give me compliments on a job well done. That praise however, came at a cost. Warnings came my way. "*Your boss feels threatened.*" "*Employees are requesting to see you for assistance rather than your coworkers.*" "*Management prefers that you coach them on personnel matters instead of seeking the advice of your boss.*"

No Thanks.

Returning to the job proposal at hand, my boss was clearly upset at my response to her offer for me to fill a higher position vacancy with no added benefits or pay. The conversation took a turn for the worst.

My boss began to ramble on with insincere and condescending observations about how nicely dressed I always was, how brightly colored my nail polish was, how well-spoken I was, how well I got along with everyone, how I needed to put in a little more time to receive more pay, etc. She offered these platitudes as reasons why I should take the more demanding position as a lateral move. In between each compliment, she would ask me again if I would accept the lateral move. My response each time was the same—"No Thanks." I felt trapped. The thoughts running through my mind were all over the place. What does this have to do with my ability to do my current job? After all, she had always given me glowing performance evaluations. What did all of this awkward flattery have to do with my ability to do the job that she had just offered me? Was it possible that regardless of how hard I had worked, or how much I had achieved, one white woman so easily distracted by my fashion choices would decide whether I deserved to be offered this or any other position as a promotion? I pretended to listen to her unclear attempts to discount my competence with ingratiation for as long as I could.

The Rejection.

At some point she must have realized that I was becoming tired of her games, because she leaned into my personal space, looked me in my eyes and said, "Kiddo, I was thinking about eliminating your position..."

And there it was. Not only did she threaten my position, she referred to me as a *child*. In that moment, the full weight of being perceived as *less than* in this woman's eyes and being counted as a *token* Black person across a white dominated company rested on my shoulders. I was alone. I was *the only Black person in every room*, including the one in which I presently sat trapped behind my desk with a gatekeeper at my door.

It's Personal.

Shortly after this humiliating encounter with my boss, I headed to the bathroom to collect myself, in hopes to be able to make it through the rest of the day. Moments later, I had received a text message from a coworker in a different department, who had seen me go into the bathroom. It read: "Your boss is acting weird. She's hanging out in the hallway outside of the bathroom, looking suspicious." Sure enough, when I opened up the bathroom door, she was strolling down the hallway. I made a stop to pick up some time sheets from a department and she popped up in that area as well. Coincidence? I don't think so.

Convinced that my boss was following me, I waited until she went on her lunch break to call one of my attorney friends. She encouraged me to go to the organization's Executive Director who made all final decisions regarding pay structure, hiring firing, etc. thus outranking my boss. My friend advised me to state only the facts of what happened and let him draw his own conclusions. I rehearsed the script of what happened over and over in my head. I was ready to go do this! Then, I started to doubt whether it was really worth it. I had seen people try to stand up against this woman and she always sought revenge and succeeded. Did I really want to go through with making a formal report and suffer the possible consequences?

Navigating Office Politics.

Fear aside, I knew that if I didn't do anything, things could get worse. Much worse. My boss had a way of getting what she wanted. I knew if I did speak up for myself, I stood a chance, albeit a small chance, that things just might get a little better. So, I found the courage to go pay the Executive Director a visit. I followed the advice of my attorney friend and stuck to the facts. To my surprise, the Executive Director, an older white gentleman, dropped everything he was doing to see me. We had already established a good working rapport. He asked what brought me in to see him that day. I closed the door behind me, and he escorted me to a private sitting area. My back was to the door that separated us from the hallway. I slowly unraveled my story. He actively listened. Halfway through, we heard a creaking noise from out in the hallway. He leaned forward in his seat and said "Shh." He got up and walked over to the door, stepped out into the hallway, came back into the room and closed the door behind him. Then, he said with a puzzled look on his face "I know you closed the door behind you before you came into my office." I later found out that when he'd left the office to inspect the noise, he discovered from his administrative assistant that my boss walked through the lobby adjacent to his office and the draft forced his office door ajar.

The executive director encouraged me to pick up where I left off. When I finished telling my story of what had happened in my office earlier that morning, his face turned beet red and he apologized for my boss's behavior. Angry, he said "No one in the organization has the authority to threaten to terminate anyone's position!" Yes, he actually confirmed that my boss had threatened to fire me, and I didn't even have to say it, sparing me from being cast and discounted as an angry Black woman.

As the day progressed, things didn't get much better. I didn't work through my lunch that day as usual. Instead, I met two friends from other departments in the breakroom, one who identified as Black and the other white. After I shared what previously happened, they both quickly consoled me and encouraged me to file a formal grievance. They each helped substantiate my concerns and told me about several occasions in which they had witnessed my boss following me. In other instances, they noticed her casual micro-aggressions, including: *"You are going to be the training lead on this project, because you are so articulate,"* and *"How do you get your hair to do that? Can I touch it?"* and the clencher, *"You people…"* apparently without drawing any attention from my white coworkers. Overall, they validated my own lived experience that she simply treated me differently than her white direct reports. Confirming this inequitable treatment through the eyes of trusted colleagues bolstered my resolve to move forward.

Collateral Damage.

In the following days, I filed my grievance with the organization's first Black General Counsel. I regret this because within a couple of weeks, my boss met him as he entered his office at 7:30 AM and presented him with a pink slip. I can't help but wonder if it was because behind the scenes, he'd pushed to do what was right to help me receive justice.

One of the two friends I confided in served as a witness for my case and provided her official statement during the investigation. As a Black woman, she suffered retaliation for her loyalty to me—but that's another story all in itself. The gist of what happened: our other white confidant turned out to be what we now call a workplace Karen. This entitled *false ally* reported our mutual Black colleague and friend for a bogus claim that was quickly dismissed, all while feigning ignorance of her actions. She also did not come to my aide as a second witness.

Neither did my coworkers in human resources (all white identified). Only one person supported me during the investigation, and I use the word investigation loosely. They assigned the investigation of my case to a young white male attorney with just a couple of weeks of experience as the Assistant General Counsel. He handled my case at face value, had all the right things to say to me, but what he said and what he had done, didn't match up. The people I had identified as witnesses were intimidated by my boss and refused to come forward. In the end, the verdict was that it was just a misunderstanding, bad management. They made my boss apologize to me. Although she never admitted any fault. Officially, it looked like nothing happened at all; there was no blemish on her personnel record. Based on the grievance outcome, the organization recommended that she work on her communication and management style. She attended a few classes and was forced to hold weekly staff meetings. Initially, I felt more like the accused, who was made to suffer alienation from my peers instead of the victim, which I really was.

Silence Was Not an Option.

Still, there was one good thing that did come out of all of this—the Executive Director, whom I'd first confided in assured me that my job was not in jeopardy and that only he had the authority to eliminate the position. A desk audit was conducted on my job duties and I ultimately received a pay increase while remaining in my current role.

The other position I was offered was posted. A white female manager was promoted from a different department with zero human resources experience to fill the vacancy. Within two years, she asked for a transfer, citing irreconcilable differences with our boss. She later confided to me that she saw how I was treated by our boss as the grievance unfolded, but she felt that she could not afford to come to my aide and speak upon my behalf because she feared she would suffer consequences. I felt betrayal and had nothing left to say to her.

There were subsequent openings in other departments that I was encouraged to apply for, and I suspect that I could have readily landed any of those positions. Honestly, my boss would have done anything just to get rid of me. Believe me, I know; she tried. But I had decided to stay in the role I was hired for, both to work on my exit strategy and more importantly, to address the *concrete wall* at that organization. I chose to become what I never had. I was a mentor for other women who looked *like me*. I helped them find white *allies* and sponsors. I led programs that offered the tools and resources they needed to successfully pursue promotion. I was their biggest cheerleader; I advocated with them in ways that got them noticed. My efforts were not in vain. I became the organization's Diversity Manager. I demanded inclusion, respect, and a seat at the table where decisions were made, policies were established, and I began to chip away at the organization's long history of systemic racism, with the help of our corporate office.

I'm not going to lie, the destructive experiences I've endured at that organization scarred me right down to my core. I walked through my work days fearful and on guard against moments of ongoing discrimination, instances of micro-aggressions, and being sidelined as a token Black person by those unable to look past the color of my skin and the paint on my nails to see the merit of my credentials and drive to get ahead for a really long time. The right opportunity for a move presented itself sometime later and I was able to leave that company for a better and more meaningful position.

Leaving that toxic environment on my own terms when the *time was right*, and not because I couldn't take it anymore, was a huge part of my own healing process. This perhaps is the strongest piece of advice that I would like to leave with other women of color faced with a similar experience.

The Next Chapter.

As a Black woman, I can never stop thinking about workplace racism. It is my Monday through Friday reality. I've learned over the years how to protect my own energy in dealing with micro-aggressive behavior in corporate America. I know that it can be especially difficult to be authentically Black in the workplace, but it is possible. I get it, Black women cannot be themselves, because the narrative has already been created for us. We are often given all of the tasks that no one else wants to tackle. We are expected to work twice as hard as everyone else, while our intelligence is ignored when promotions are handed out. We are seen as the *angry Black woman* when we ask why we are treated this way.

If your story is like mine, and you've already seen the writing on the wall. There are actionable things that you can do to make your last few weeks, months or years a little more bearable until you can find a new job. Here are some tips:

- *Set boundaries for yourself.* In hindsight, it really wasn't a good idea to work through breaks. Go ahead and enjoy lunch with a close friend. Go outside on your break and enjoy some fresh air.
- *Find trusted allies in key positions.*
- *Find a good support system outside of work:* Have friends or family you can vent to and confide in about what you are going through at work.
- *Don't internalize the misperceptions of others.*
- *Invest in self-care:* Treat yourself to a spa day or take up a hobby.
- *Pay it forward:* Be a mentor.

- *Don't mourn traitors*; Step over them and move on!
- *Leave when the time is right.* Leave for a better career or become an entrepreneur.

And for our white allies...

- *Be Willing to Learn.* If you truly want to support your Black coworkers, we encourage you to seek out on your own, knowledge about our history, culture, challenges and movements. Learn about the Black experience, even if it makes you feel uncomfortable.
- *Get Uncomfortable.* Acknowledge your privilege. This is not an attack. This is not about you. Stand with Black colleagues regardless of personal cost. We need to be able to *trust* you. Acknowledge past mistakes that the organization allowed. Determine ways to correct past injustices, including but not limited to workplace culture and pay disparities between Black and white employees.
- *Speak Up.* Be proactive and draw attention to your Black colleague's contributions so that their ideas are not overlooked. Examine your hiring, evaluation, promotion, training, and pay structures to ensure that they are fair and inclusive.
- *Be More Than a Mentor; Be a Sponsor.* Mentoring is good. Sponsoring is better. The role of mentors is to give advice and assist the mentee in navigating the organization's cultural and social norms. True advocacy means putting your reputation on the line even at your own expense. Sponsors recommend Black colleagues for jobs and promotions.
- *Don't Be Afraid to Have Difficult Conversations.* Don't wait for us to file a grievance. Microaggressions are really not all that *micro* for those of us on the receiving end. Microaggressions deserve to be noticed and challenged *every day*, directly with the aggressor and systemically.

Didn't You Get the Memo

....

Nicole F. Smith, MBA

THE DAY I was called an *Uncle Tom* by someone that looked like me made me evaluate myself, my fight for racial equality, and my leadership style not as a female, but as a Black female. As a Black woman in the corporate world, there is a long list of items we have to maneuver through – it's a jungle out there. As a female, there is a somewhat quiet battle against my male counterpart, convincing him that I am assertive, not aggressive, and passionate, not emotional. As a female–a Black female in the workplace–there is a crab in the barrel type of mentality against the other females in the workplace. There is a different level of exhaustion that takes over when constantly having to remind the other woman of color that you're not her competition and would rather present a unified force to create a movement together for equality and parity. If she is a white woman, at times, you wonder where the sisterhood is at all. Minda Harts, the author of *The Memo*, states that "People are not used to seeing us in positions that require us to lead." Referring to "Black females." Sadly, the discrimination and prejudice in the workplace between genders or from a different race is disappointing and somewhat expected, however experiencing same-race discrimination can affect the heart and soul differently.

I have lived in the corporate world for over twenty years. I considered it an experience and then I changed the label from 'experience' to 'journey' during the fifteenth year. This was a mindset shift as an experience is judged in length versus a journey being viewed as getting from one place to another. I was on a journey of getting from just a job to my real purpose. On this journey, I reported to many different leaders with many different leadership styles. Only two of these leaders were Black– and they were both women. You would think I had learned a lot – I did! These two women had very different styles. One was compassionate, encouraging, and empathetic to all of her employees, teaching me how to treat other people of all races who were part of our team. It encouraged the team to bring their best selves to work and perform at their best. The other woman was extremely authoritative and believed in tough love. She chastised all her employees publicly, especially the African Americans. Privately, the behavior was explained as "it is hard out there for us, so the lessons will be harder for you." Today, I recognized that the way she treated her employees, especially her Black employees, was not tough love, but her hard lessons were on how to conform to white corporate America and make sure they'd like us. This might have been my first experience with same-race discrimination in the corporate world, I just didn't know it at the time.

Have I faced discrimination or racism within the corporate world? Yes, mostly in the form of microaggressions. Have I missed out on promotions or upward movement due to the color of my skin? Yes, but it may not have been noticed until after the fact – after I decided it was time to leave because, well, there was no room for growth.

I persevered being very intentional in the roles I chose. As I became wiser to the game that had to be played, I treated everyone fairly as a leader, but made sure that a wider net was cast when it came time to recruit, interview, promote or provide special projects. I have also been intentional in making sure that we, as African American women, were at the table. Attempting to do this has pissed off many people, but in the fight for equality and equity, there will always be pissed off people. I had to choose courage over comfort as you cannot have both.

In a particular Fortune 500 company, I was excited but nervous about starting a new role. Word on the street was that they were somewhat dysfunctional in certain departments. After having to deal with other organizations and continuously fight to prove my value and worth, I was looking for an organization where I could pack away my boxing gloves and thrive. But I later realized I had to carry them in my purse every day, but not for obvious opponents.

As soon as I walked in the door of this new employer, I was embraced by my team and other Black colleagues. The Black executives, however, felt that they had to have a façade for appearance purposes. I later determined that this was the culture. I wondered if they were conforming to the white corporate world. I will never know.

A couple of weeks in, I was approached by a Black colleague who reported to a peer of mine. She wanted to have a meeting. It was what the vice president of the department called a "get to know you" type of meeting. This Black female employee and I, we can call her Stephanie, were both new to this organization. However, I was a team leader she was going to work closely with, and she was an individual contributor. I was game. My attitude was, "Come on, sis, let's talk." After a few fun questions, the first serious question was, "As a leader what are you going to do to help the Black employees in the department?" The abrupt question threw me off for a second. I later found out, she asked the same question of the white, female vice president of the department, and with the same intensity.

As I have moved up in the corporate world working different

leadership positions, I was occasionally approached with, "*How will you help me, my sista?*" A mentor told me that as I moved up that it was coming! I am an advocate for diversity and inclusion and very active and intentional in diversifying the workplace, the department, even down to my team with all races, all genders and talents identified.

There is one caveat – I will mentor, support, and promote individuals based on their talent, skills, and even potential, but not on race alone...not solely because you "look like me." Being a Black female leader does not mean that I will automatically give another Black female the keys to the car and house. I will never forget when Barack Obama became the 44th president. Some members of the Black culture forgot he was President of the United States, making decisions for the people – not "just the Black people." For there to be a test given *only* to Black leaders with the expectation to only "bring up" the Black people for that passing grade – well, I think many of us will fail in more than one way if we are true leaders.

As I was asked this question by Stephanie, "As a leader what are you going to do to help the Black employees in the department?" I quickly went to the mindset of "good intent." I thought for a quick second that this woman was comfortable with me, and she wanted to know that as a Black female leader, what was I going to do to make sure "the culture was looked after and had a seat at the table." Okay! Honest question, but still quite assertive, but so am I.

As the months went by, I did have to deal with my direct manager, a white female, and as time went on, I had determined that she was very intimidated by me. There were several petty things she did to sabotage my growth and relationships within the organization, but I couldn't prove that it had anything to do with race...and that was frustrating. It appeared that I was just another female, "showing her up," who just happened to be

Black. After conversations with the vice president of the entire department, my complaints along with those of my other teammates, in addition to her insufficient performance, were instrumental in this manager eventually being removed.

After this occurrence, Stephanie attempted to have casual conversations with me regarding my former manager and share the trouble she had with her. She also indicated that with this manager being gone, it was now more critical for me to "do my thing," and show the vice president what I could do, especially as a Black woman. A Black female team member approached me after she saw Stephanie and I having a conversation and said, "I won't say much, but be careful of Stephanie. She seems like she has an agenda, but I can't put my finger on it."

I observed how interestingly Stephanie floated through the department having "get to know you" meetings with colleagues. She gained quick friendships with other Black females in the office who were also individual contributors. As part of the leadership team, I would participate in casual water cooler chats or "what did you do this past weekend" type of conversations. Whenever a Black female executive was promoted or praised, she would go around and tell other Black females that we should get a congratulatory card for them with all of our signatures. But the kicker was that I would be the sender of the card since I was the Black leader in our department. Stephanie would even tell me "good job" when we hired other Black female colleagues stating, "Black girl magic." Stephanie also volunteered herself to be the department's unofficial book club's organizer, with the first book being *The Memo* by Minda Harts.

After hearing of the unofficial book club, I decided to have a conversation with Stephanie's manager and the vice president because I had a gut feeling that there was a "mean-girl clique" forming with the Black female colleagues in the department. I could sense that when decisions were made for the department and Stephanie was not happy about it. She would gather her group together for them to discuss privately. I wasn't privy to those conversations, and yes, I was Black, but I was also on the leadership team. I shared with my vice president and Stephanie's manager only after the vice president stated that she had a feeling that something was brewing in the department. I simply asked the vice president if she had read *The Memo* and advised that she should, as it is a good book, but it also provides context as to why I had shared my intuition. I shared that this book was being read by the Black female colleagues and that it could go two ways: The attitude of "this organization is not giving Black women a seat at the table, and we will storm the village" and make demands without any discussions or "what can we as Black women do to show we are supposed to be at the table, have earned our seat at the table and take our seat." To this day, I am not sure if the vice president read the book or not.

Fast forward two months. I had now been with the organization for approximately eight months. Stephanie had made it known about decisions she disagreed with that were made for the department, but she made these complaints to the other Black females in the department, not to leadership. I, however, heard some of them loud and clear, and some under muffled whispers.

This was when I had to bring my boxing gloves in, metaphorically speaking, for a purpose. I could have never imagined. Never in a million years, would I have thought another Black female would question my "loyalty" to the Black culture. In these times, where the Black community is striving to have solidarity in an attempt to come together with allies and remove systemic barriers, insinuating that an individual is an Uncle Tom and not having "the receipts" or proof as they say, can have hard consequences, especially when the individual placing the blame is another person of color.

This unfortunate situation played out like this – it involved a white male, who we will call John, and you guessed it, Stephanie.

John was a member of my team, an individual contributor. The drama had been taking place for some time unbeknownst to me or Stephanie's manager. All the typical team performance management tasks were taking place, such as having team meetings, one on ones, project updates, stakeholder updates, etc. There did not appear to be any discord in the situation. John stated that he didn't feel that Stephanie really understood what she was supposed to do on the project. He continued to state that at the depth she was going into the project which was unnecessary, and he was being asked to do things on the project that didn't make sense based on the client's requirements.

A piece of material for the project was shared with me, and to be honest, I had to agree with John. The content Stephanie provided did not contain the desired outcomes or desired points to deliver a finished product. I sent an email to Stephanie stating that John didn't understand his tasks to help her. John also shared with me that Stephanie had blown up on him in an earlier incident, stormed off, and stated she would do it herself. With that said, the email included the question, "Do you still need John's help?" Stephanie showed up to work late that day, approached me angrily and stated how "pissed off she was," and that I had not received the whole story. However, she didn't provide the whole story. Instead she decided to work at another location for the rest of the day.

Later that same evening, there was an attempt by Stephanie to get ahead of the situation. I received inappropriate texts from her with quotes from Minda Hart's book (Chapter 8 to be specific: No More Passes: For My White Readers) in an attempt to make me her ally, to "sista-girl" me, for me to grab my pitchfork and storm the village. Honestly, I wasn't too sure of the intent. This chapter was used to demonstrate that she wouldn't have been able to drop the ball, disrupt projects, miss deadlines, and paint herself as a misunderstood and confused employee. She continued with the text to state that accountability and integrity are the more significant issues in this regard, and John had wasted valuable time with the accusation and that because he was white, he was getting a pass. I was offended. I had to be very careful in my text back to her. The only reply was, "Okay, Stephanie."

The next morning, I showed the text to Stephanie's manager, wondering if I'd missed something about this project. He was disappointed for her lack of respect and knew nothing of what Stephanie stated was taking place. Stephanie's manager and I decided it would be best to have a joint meeting with her to understand what was going on with the project, what help she needed, and how we could support her. We did let her know that we were not aware of any issues until now. We also requested specifics regarding what was done wrong or not to the client's satisfaction so we could help.

Stephanie began to tell us how John disappointed her, how he was no help, and how he needed to be punished for wasting her time. She actually wanted to see John punished. Stephanie went on to state, "Because a person of color would never get away with this."–yet she failed to communicate what *"this"* was. Again, we had asked why she hadn't approached the leaders sooner to step in and help remove obstacles for her. It was stated that, as leaders, we should have known what was going on – yet she and John, both, failed to communicate the details. She again asked how John was going to be punished "Because if it was a Black employee, *this* would never happen. I would never receive special attention." I was confused. I squared up and asked her if she thought I was giving my employee John "a pass" because he was white. *And* when I asked if she really thought this – I got a shoulder shrug. What in the world? Allegations were made, and I wanted to hear her thoughts behind them. She gave none.

Neither John nor Stephanie, had met the expectations of what we think are standard competencies of a team member such as communication, decision making, problem-solving, collaborating, etc. Stephanie took absolutely zero accountability. In fact – the blame was equally placed on the leaders.

Did we speak with John as well? Yes. John had stated to me, "I could've done better handling this project, and I see why she might have been frustrated. However, there are pieces to this story that are missing, as I wasn't fully aware of what she needed and how to move forward as she failed to communicate clearly or at times, not at all. I do not think she understood her role. I should have brought it to you sooner." We had agreed on how to move forward on the next project and how to avoid similar conflicts next time. Also, there was no mention of race, punishment, or bias regarding her being a woman or a Black woman. It was disappointing.

Here's the thing–history has shown that the race card was invented as a way to pacify the Black community in thinking they had a "card" to play in this race game. However, if misused or used carelessly, the person playing the card, loses in more ways than one. Here is what I say: If you are going to use the race card, slam it on the table like the big joker at the end of a spades game (inside Black culture thing). Can I honestly admit that this was said to Stephanie? Yes, I had said it. Whether right or wrong, I wanted her to truly understand where I was coming from.

The strange thing is that she didn't actually say "Uncle Tom" (yet, she'd made it very clear.) But she did feel that some sort of favor was given to John. I won't take that feeling away...of course, she couldn't say what that favor was. Again...no receipts.

There are performance expectations set in the workplace for all team members – no matter their race or gender- at least for my team members. And these expectations were not met. After the situation was brought to my attention, this was addressed as any typical workplace performance issue.

In the end, there was no favor given to John. I do have a

background in Human Resources; however, I did consult with my Human Resources (HR) Representative for guidance as I wanted to have things on record. I wanted to give HR a heads up in case Stephanie had gone to HR first. See, the difference between Stephanie and me is that I knew her background. She clearly didn't know mine. The HR Representative stated that I'd done everything I was supposed to do. They'd appreciated me bringing the situation to their attention as soon as I'd been aware of what was taking place and, for providing the proper updates.

A Black female team member was involved, a white male team member was involved, and a new book called "The Memo" was being highly promoted among the Black women team members. A perfect storm, right? Yet, this beautiful blend was used as an evil potion, to create a situation that had nothing to do with race but everything to do with an individual who was frustrated by their lack of knowledge and inability to handle a project. Instead of using this as an opportunity to learn and garner help, Stephanie went down the wrong path to try and gain an "ally" and when I didn't punish the white team member, she decided to make accusations of same-race discrimination. I could tell that she had gained the other Black female colleagues as allies as they spoke less to me or hushed up quickly whenever I'd walk by. My vice president was made aware of the situation by Stephanie's manager and offered to speak with Stephanie. I stated that she could do what she wanted to do because unbeknownst to her I was moving on to another opportunity to focus on my business.

I was "sista-girled" for the first time as a leader...as a Black female leader, and when that didn't work, Stephanie wanted to make the situation about race when her competencies were challenged. Stephanie decided to *Uncle Tom* me...and that hurt me to my core.

Closed Door Opportunities

Ruby

BEING AN AMBITIOUS Black woman in higher education has been a rough road. From experiencing the trials that come with being the first woman in my family to obtain a master's degree before the age of forty, to climbing the corporate ladder to become a full time, business professor, it hasn't been easy. Through the years, I've learned that with every opportunity comes roadblocks, but when you are a Black woman, a few can somehow turn into a lot.

In my previous position working as an Executive Assistant for a community college in the Midwest, I was denied several opportunities to advance in my career by my white supervisor. At first, she seemed genuine and appeared excited about me working, even going so far stating she wanted me to advance in my career and move up within the college. I was lured in with her charm and believing that she was different and truly wanted me to succeed, I made the mistake of sharing my aspirations with her of wanting to become a part-time professor in the business department at the college. Having earned a Master's Degree in Business Administration, I was qualified to teach business courses and she knew this. Again, she expressed that she was fully supportive for my goals, or so it seemed.

During the spring of 2020, I was presented with an opportunity to teach an evening course in the business department. I'm not one to sit around and wait for things to just happen, I had been in constant contact with the dean of the business department, always inquiring about teaching opportunities. This position had come with me getting out there, networking and letting key players know what my intent was. So, when I was finally offered the opportunity to teach a small business management course for twelve weeks I was beyond excited! With all my paperwork turned in, I began to prepare for the course by looking at the instructional materials on Blackboard when suddenly, out of nowhere, my supervisor informed me that I could not teach the course because according to her "It would interfere with my current position at the college." I was angry. "How could she do this to me?" I immediately began to investigate what she had shared with me, starting with the employee handbook. To my surprise, there were no policies that stated full time employees could not teach part-time at the college. In addition to there not being any written policies, there were numerous full-time staff members at the college who had taught one or two classes during the evening hours, after they had finished their full-time position duties. My anger eventually turned to pain, with me privately crying in front of the dean of the business department. She was just as surprised as I was to learn my supervisor would not allow me to teach the course.

Now if that wasn't enough, hold tight, because there were other incidents where opportunities for me to advance in my career were blocked by this same supervisor. After denying me the opportunity to teach part-time, when I presented an opportunity to attend a training that I felt would help me in my position, she denied that, too. I had learned about a Title IX investigator training and felt that attending would allow me to sharpen my skills and learn how to give more attention to details that are often overlooked when doing employment verifications and background checks in the onboarding process for internal and external candidates. When I had shared these sentiments with my supervisor, she stated that she would think about it. I later learned that she had scheduled two of my white coworkers for the same training.

One day while talking to my Black coworker who was the Title IX Coordinator, about the training, she informed me that my supervisor decided not to send me to the training because she needed me to supervise the main desk. "What? You can't be serious!" I could not believe this was happening to me again! There were at least ten other people in the office who could have supervised the desk in my absence for two days and nine of them were white! This was entirely too much but wait...it doesn't end there.

Due to the COVID-19 pandemic, I was furloughed from my job at the end of May 2020. When my supervisor and I spoke via video chat, she was very short and direct. I had also noticed that she never mentioned how long I would be furloughed from my job. I was no longer surprised by her nor her actions. I believe that God closes doors in our lives to make room for new and better opportunities to present themselves.

With all the trials I had experienced in that position, many would have given up, but I didn't. I continued to press forward and was eventually blessed with a part-time, online adjunct professor position. In addition, I was offered the opportunity to work as an instructional designer. I now know that none of this would have been possible had I not remained strong, motivated, and humble.

As a Black woman, there are several pieces of advice I would like to give to the person reading this. Firstly, never give up on your dreams! God will bless you wholeheartedly if you have faith in Him and in yourself. Second, remember to always put

God first in your life and have faith and patience when going after your personal and career goals. And lastly, surround yourself with positive people. Don't allow negative people, whether family, friends or your supervisor to steal your joy because they will bring you down and make you lose sight of the glory with which God has intended to bless you. Being an ambitious Black woman comes with numerous roadblocks, but when you have unshakable faith, you can overcome anything and be successful in whatever you pursue.

Refuse To Play It Safe

....

Von M. Griggs-Laws

I AM VON; born and raised in St. Louis, Missouri. I'm the middle child of five children that shared our upbringing in a home with both parents present. Considered a middle class family, living in the city, life was good. My parents had eighth and eleventh grade educations and were from Macon, MS. When it came to school, as we learned, in many ways we became our parent's educators. They felt it was important that we knew how life was for them while living in the deep South, because regardless of if we were long gone, we were still growing up in the Jim Crow era. My dad worked for the City of St. Louis and would often take us to different neighborhoods and restaurants to *"See how other people lived,"* he would say. Momma was a domestic technician for a prominent doctor and was big on helping everybody.

When the Civil Rights movement began to take place in the country, there was a huge concern for us, Black folks, to still be respectful to white people. It was respect out of fear and knowing when to "play it safe." My parents also made sure we understood the importance of hard work, showing respect, and being kind to others, which became a staple characteristic for each of their children.

We were fortunate to live in a mixed neighborhood which consisted of Blacks, whites and a few Jewish families, too. I attended and graduated from the first integrated public high school in the city, and it was during our work study classes that we received visits from military recruiters. I took an interest in the US Air Force, yet it was a few years before I would enlist. I'd worked since the age of sixteen in the hospitality and manufacturing industries and both were very diverse in race, ethnicity, gender and age. So, when I was laid off from my manufacturing job, I remembered the Air Force recruiter saying; "The Air Force is more accepting of females than the Army." I believed him and enlisted.

My Dad was concerned about my wellbeing and didn't want me to join the military, but I saw it as a way out. Home life was good most days, but there were enough toxic times that gave me the inner courage to finally leave home. It took some convincing for my parents, especially my dad. He wanted to make sure that I would be okay and survive the military. I thought my experiences with other races up until that point had prepared me to understand the true differences. I also knew that if all else failed, I'd just "play it safe." My dad believed that since the crime rate had increased in St. Louis, if I had told people I was from the city, they would back down from troubling me, boy was he wrong.

During my time in the Air Force, I experienced many occurrences of discrimination; race, religion and gender. Thinking back, the first indication that I may have encountered some difficulties due to the color of my skin was during basic training. It was during this time that all branches of the military were introduced to the Secretary of Defense Title 10, US code 481; which spells out forms of discrimination and a zero-tolerance policy. Why was this necessary you might ask? Historically, the military had been seen as the "white man's institution," and my experiences would prove that to be true.

My earliest recollection of discrimination was from a civilian supervisor while I was in the U.S. Air Force Academy. In an effort to protect the guilty, we will refer to him as "Mr. N." Our

Air Force 35-10 Dress & Appearance Regulation had recently changed the verbiage in its policy regarding hair. It had been changed from the wearing of a braid to braids. Excited, I hurried and had my hair braided and while it met the standard of no more than three inches thick, Mr. N and many others thought it was too controversial and that I was flaunting my "Blackness." This resulted in me having to meet with my First Sergeant and several other leaders to discuss the intent of my interpretation of the new standard and if there was a possible typo or error. It took approximately three weeks for this matter to be settled by headquarters. When the dust settled, Mr. N didn't talk to me for months. Imagine working with a supervisor that doesn't talk to you, but instead communicates with you through others, email, or maybe not at all. I was beginning to realize that playing it safe may not be an option while I served in the military, so to protect myself, I reported him to our section chief, Mrs. S, who was an African American civilian.

She asked me to remain peaceful and to remove my braids until the investigation was complete. "Really?" A Black woman was really asking me to "play it safe?" She refused to support me, and I saw her as a sell-out. I decided not to play it safe this time, and I kept wearing my braids. My actions resulted in me being reassigned to the evening/weekend shift with Wednesdays & Thursdays as my off days. This was pivotal in my home life because though I was married, my daughter was enrolled in a daycare center that closed at 6 PM and her father worked evenings from 3-12 PM. I knew this reassignment was to give me less exposure to the other cadet students and base personnel. For the first time since the birth of my daughter, I found myself seeking out a personal babysitter to watch her in the evenings. Dismayed, I filed a discrimination complaint. I knew I was not being allowed to have a normal rotating shift like my two coworkers because I had decided to not play it safe. Three weeks later, a memo was sent command-wide supporting the new hairstyle policy. I was cleared of being out of regulation and needless to say, braiding hair for other Airmen became my side hustle. "God had a ram in the bush."

My second discrimination experience had more to do with me being a woman than my race. I was stationed in England with high rotations and long days. My three peers and supervisor were from the Southern states of Alabama, Georgia and South Carolina. Our facility had one restroom for a total of seven people on staff. As I worked, I often overheard comments like, "Women should not be in combat." One thought that women in the military were taking jobs from men who wanted to provide for their families. I wish I could say this was the attitude of just men. One of their spouses actually had the audacity to warn me "Not to entice her husband during field exercises." Woah…really? She had no idea of the hell I was being put through and her husband was the least of my concerns. I should have felt safe in this space, but I didn't.

As time went on, I refused to accept the sly remarks and vulgar comments. When my colleagues would defecate in the toilet and refuse to practice sanitation and hygiene by simply flushing it, I complained. I began to request respect and demanded that they clean the bathroom after each use. When it didn't happen, I complied by using the restroom at other facilities and offices. It wasn't as bad as Katherine Johnson in the movie *Hidden Figures*, but it was enough.

Though I was not a junior ranking Airman, I was still assigned unfavorable units to inspect and flight-line watch, which meant longer inspections and longer hours. By then, I was a divorced mother of now two daughters. The daycare situation was the same, with this center closing at 6 PM, too. So here I was once again, forced to seek out people to watch my children after hours. Sometimes, there was no one available on short notice and there were occasions when I had to leave my children secured in my office while I responded to occurring incidents. I was surely blessed and watched over by God, because that was illegal, however, I was forced to make those decisions at that time. The way I saw it, those men had wives to take care of their children. I didn't want special treatment and I didn't have the extra support that they had–and they knew this. In the end, all I wanted was fairness, equality and respect. After all, that's what the government had promised me. Sorry mom and dad, but I could no longer just take the abuse and "play it safe."

When I informed my section chief of what was taking place, he assured me he would have a talk with my colleagues but warned me about being "too sensitive." With that complaint, the fires against me were turned up higher. Suddenly, I started having headaches on Sunday nights, before going onto base on Monday mornings. The nausea I felt, the weight loss and hair thinning from the stress increased exponentially. Then there was the documenting of conversations and incidents which I needed in order to build a case. All of this took a toll on me.

The country was in peacetime, but I felt like I was in a domestic war zone. Another ram in the bush would come in the form of Major C; a newly assigned Security Force Commander to our installation, another African American female. I got to conduct her base introduction one-on-one. Over time, she became a mentor and shared a few of her learned tips from her personal arsenal. The two of us bonded and built a dialogue over our shared experiences with racial hostility in the workplace. She gave me tangible tips on becoming better and not bitter, knowing that the incidents I was going through at that time and had endured in the past were building strength and character within me. I continued to refuse to stay quiet and just "play it safe." I later filed an Equal Opportunity Complaint with Social Actions. Again, this was stressful because of the documentation that was involved. This went on for an entire month as I continued to build a case file regarding the discrimination that I'd been experiencing. In the end, it all paid off as my three peers received counseling, discrimination training and letters of reprimand. When it came time for my re-enlistment, I chose Major C for the honor of performing my ceremony rather than my own commander and that did not sit well with my colleagues.

After retiring from the military, I moved to the Dallas VA Medical Center. I was literally the new chick, or should I say, the only chick on the block. I was the only female amongst fourteen men. I learned early on in this assignment, that although this was a new environment, and they were Black male veterans, many of their behaviors were similar to my past experiences of sexism and intimidation. Often, I would question myself. I was the only common denominator in every situation, was it something I was doing wrong?

Soon my work was being sabotaged. Week after week there was something new. They played games that consisted of busting the locks on my storage areas and stealing equipment that had been assigned to me. I honestly expected more support from these men than I'd ever been offered from any white man in my career. There were a few who genuinely respected me and my knowledge, but the others did not.

We had a huge inspection by several local and state politicians and once again, my crew of seven subordinates could not complete their assignments because the equipment was mysteriously moved out of my section. Once again, I could no longer "play it safe." If I wanted to keep my job and be a good leader, I knew I had to fight for my crew. I had to take the risk and speak up. I filed an EEO complaint with the Union.

The investigation lasted over two years. Eventually, I could no longer trust anyone. The entire department eventually had to undergo civility and leadership training and I was blamed because the money to cover these expenses came from our department's operating budget. I was saddened because no concern was shown for my emotional well-being and the poor performance ratings. This was truly a lonely, heart wrenching time. Peers and subordinates stopped talking to me. Throughout the medical center, I was labeled the "bitch" or "ole girl." Once again, I found myself documenting everything. Until then, there had not been another female to hold these men accountable for their actions. Every conversation I had was now being scrutinized. I wasn't always informed of meetings that would have a direct impact on my work. Only five of the fourteen men supported me and two had written witness statements on my behalf.

My case was eventually settled in Federal Court on the bases of gender discrimination. I was awarded a decent monetary settlement and a lapel pin for dedicated service. My direct supervisor, also a Black man was reassigned from his position for failure to act on my initial complaint with the Union and the additional costs of time, money and morale of the department. From the heavens above, I know my parents are proud of my achievements. Through many life struggles, I've heard their voices comforting me in times of despair. I've taken on battles that they never would have during their generation. Respect, kindness and playing it safe to them often meant tolerating injustice, something I wasn't willing to do. It's important that we don't always "play it safe" when we see or experience injustice. We can no longer be silent due to fear of retaliation. We have to be willing to take risks, even when dangerous, knowing that our actions will eventually spark change.

Algorithms, Audits and Black Women

Emily Edwards

MY COMPANY WAS a private mental health agency located in Lake County, Indiana, established in 2004. We specialized in the treatment of the severely mentally ill. It is important to note that my company which primarily provided services to African Americans was one of three out of the ten mental health agencies in Lake County, Indiana that was owned by a Black woman generating six-figures in revenue. Mental illness healthcare is a giant part of the gross domestic product (GDP) of the United States – approximately twenty percent. Private insurance handles approximately thirty-four percent of the total cost, while Medicare takes on twenty percent, and Medicaid seventeen percent, and the rest is paid some other way. My company was a Medicaid/Medicare provider. Each claim that was submitted contained a number of codes that described the type of services being provided to the patient. Note–patient records can become a treasure trove and claim-based algorithms are frequently used by the different payees to identify various factors like race. During my time as the owner of a mental health agency, there were frequent audits that often left me making difficult choices about how to best use my resources when defending provided services and fighting the claim denials that followed, I didn't understand back then that many of the obstacles that I faced were the result of biased algorithms.

Biases can be introduced into algorithms in multiple ways. Whatever method is used, it requires human decisions on how the data is categorized as well as which data is included or discarded. Keep in mind, algorithms are only as impartial as the individual who designed and programmed them. Research by Obermeyer (2019) found evidence of racial bias in one widely used algorithm in the medical system. Black patients were assigned the same level of risk by the algorithm, yet were sicker than white patients. The authors estimated that this racial bias reduced the number of Black patients identified for extra care. These biases occurred because the algorithms used health costs as a proxy for health needs. The algorithm was programmed to produce data that indicated less money was spent on Black patients who had the same level of need as white patients. As a result of this biased programming of the algorithm, false results concluded that Black patients were healthier than the equally ill white patients. These biases could be corrected by the removal of cost as a proxy to predict what race would need extra care.

In 2012, my company received a letter from Indiana Medicaid stating we were being audited again. This was the fourth audit that had been conducted within the 8 years I had been in business as a mental health agency. When an audit is received, a time frame to submit all documentation is given. So, with this in mind, I began gathering the requested documentation and submitted everything in a timely manner. After the submission, I expected to get a response within three months, but I never received one. I reached out to the audit department several times and was informed they were running behind and I would receive a letter once a decision had been rendered. So, I continued to run my company and never really gave it much thought, even after the three-month time period had passed. After the first audit, I assumed this was normal protocol for Medicaid. However; after the fourth audit, I began to notice that the more my agency grew, the frequency of the audits increased. It should also be noted that Caucasian individuals who lacked the knowledge of the services that were provided by my agency conducted each of these audits. I also noticed that these audits were being conducted on all mental health agencies in the area that were owned by Black women.

Fast forward to the summer of 2016. In June of that year, I received a letter from the State of Indiana Medical Licensing Board under which I was practicing, informing me that they had suspended my agency's medical director's psychiatric license. In the State of Indiana, a social worker in private practice cannot bill Medicaid without the supervision of a licensed psychiatrist. So, as a result, I had to put my billing on hold until I could find another psychiatrist, but we continued to provide services to our clients. This meant no money was coming into my agency.

Little did I know, this was the beginning of the end of a business I had put my all into growing; which also had been my only source of income. I watched helplessly in horror as it was slowly snatched away from me. My emotions were all over the place, vacillating between anger and feelings of failure. I also began to realize that none of my peers in the mental health profession were willing to testify on my behalf. As I tried to maintain a positive attitude while providing services to severely mentally ill clients, figuring out where my next meal was coming from began to cause me to experience severe insomnia, along with bouts of depression.

Then there was the lingering audit. Remember the audit from Indiana Medicaid, I'd mentioned earlier; the one I never received a response to regarding the final outcome. Well, Indiana Medicaid finally sent me a response in July 2016. It took them four years to tell me I owed $20,000. My first thought was to just pay it. My mother always told me to go with my first mind. Nevertheless, I second guessed myself and took advice from someone I shouldn't have and appealed the decision. I would later come to regret that.

Approximately two weeks after the appeal was filed, I received a visit from the Attorney General of the Medicaid Fraud Unit. The day they walked into my office I had a full-blown panic attack. Consciously, I knew what was happening but subconsciously, this felt like a nightmare that would never end. Just knowing in my mind that I had not done anything wrong and to have to keep explaining the operations of my business to someone who had the power to close it, made me sick to my stomach. I was informed that the purpose of their visit stemmed from the appeal I had filed.

The Attorney General (AG) said they would have to conduct an audit as well because it appeared that I was double billing. The AG also validated that their system employed algorithms, which flagged codes that were used repeatedly. As I'd revealed earlier, these algorithms can contain identifiers that indicate the race of the provider treating the clients. They informed me the system showed I used the same CPT codes on a consistent basis, so this triggered the system to perform an audit on my billing. I found it appalling that machines increasingly made decisions that impacted human life and big organizations — particularly in mental health care —to leverage massive data sets in ways that run the risk of automating racism or other human biases. During the AG visit, I found myself having to explain the operations of my business once again. This was even more aggravating as they were the same individuals that had conducted the last audit. It was just downright disturbing to me to be audited by someone that didn't have a clue about what they were auditing. The AG appeared genuine in their effort of wanting to assist me in resolving this matter, but how could they have given me assistance when they did not comprehend the process. Despite no wrongdoings found in each audit, my company continued to be audited for the same CPT codes. I asked for an explanation for the frequency in audits, but the AG did not provide a logical explanation. They instead informed me that their prior audit on me four years earlier did not find any wrongdoings. They'd also informed me that after receiving the request from the Medicaid Fraud Unit for this audit to be conducted, they were not under the impression the results would have produced anything different from the previous audits.

I was angry and frustrated as to why I had to address two different audits. Why was my life being disrupted by an algorithm? Based on the fact that the algorithms had been programmed to identify my race as a provider, no evidence of wrongdoings had been found. The frequency of audits, as it became glaringly apparent, had more to do with my race and the race of the clients to which I provided services. Yes, I was a victim of corporate racism.

I willingly cooperated and provided the business documentation requested of me. At this point, I was doing my best to remain hopeful this nightmare would end soon, hoping I would be able to continue with my practice. I had also found another psychiatrist and we were now able to resume billing, or so I thought. Boy, was I wrong!

In August of 2016, the final blow was issued to me. I received a letter from Medicaid informing me that my company was being placed on payment suspension effective immediately. This letter is permanently ingrained in my memory. I felt as if the rug had been pulled from underneath me and I was unable to regain my balance. My chest was tight, and I literally could not breathe. At that moment, I concluded I would not be able to handle this on my own, so I decided to hire an attorney who specialized in this area. By now, I was a basket case and I honestly was no longer able to make logical decisions.

The legal services were not cheap. The first meeting I had with the attorney lasted for more than an hour. The retainer was

$10,000. I cried during the entire meeting. The attorney assured me that based on what I had told them, my case seemed fairly simple and should not take long to resolve. This statement proved to be incorrect. This was just the beginning of increased anxiety, feelings of hopelessness and realizing that a career that I loved could possibly end in the blink of an eye.

During this time, I started researching how many other mental health providers in private practice were being audited by Indiana Medicaid and the frequency. The results were interesting to say the least. Remember, I told you my business was located in Northwest Indiana. The socio-economic makeup of this area is predominantly African American working class and the majority of service providers in this area at the time were also African Americans. My findings indicated this area was audited more than any other county located in the State of Indiana. A meeting with my attorney's office confirmed this. After I signed the contract with my attorneys, they began communication with the AG and the attorneys with the Medicaid Fraud Unit, but their efforts were no better than mine. They did not provide my attorney's office with any evidence that proved I had committed fraud. They did, however; request a plethora of additional documentation from me. I was defending myself without seeing the evidence being used against me. This was how due process worked and it surely wasn't justice. According to my attorney, Medicaid had this kind of power and was not obligated to share any information with me. Unfortunately for me, this was their idea of due process.

I spent the rest of 2016 providing documentation, which was redundant most of the time, to the AG and the Medicaid fraud unit. Every time I provided the documentation requested, I would receive another request for more information or to explain what I had sent to them. It really began to feel as if I had been singled out. I had slowly depleted my savings and retirement accounts to pay for legal fees and my case was still not resolved. I also noticed I was being watched on social media by staff from the Indiana Medicaid agency. I concluded that racism was still alive and well, but more covert and modernized in the form of algorithms and resources that were supposed to help people instead of hurting them.

There were many days that I'd wonder how much longer I could take this. I also knew in my heart that if not for the grace of God, I would have just given up. I am sure you are saying to yourself how much longer could this go on? Well, guess what, the puzzle had another piece. In December 2016, while sitting in my office, there was a knock at the door. Before I could say come in, the door opened, and it was the AG...again. I just threw my hands up in the air out of sheer exhaustion and said, "I cannot do this. I am leaving, and if you need further information, please contact my attorney." As I prepared to leave the AG said to me, "We are not here to investigate you, but another individual that did contract work for you." I reluctantly agreed to speak with them. I was informed that they were investigating this individual for fraud and wanted copies of my records during the time this individual was a 1099 Contractor for my company. This person of interest was also a Black woman. I provided the records that they requested and assured them I had no other dealings with this professional. I was hoping this would be the only involvement I would have in this matter. Once again, my assumption was wrong.

Charges were later filed against this professional and not only did I get a subpoena from a Federal Public Defender, but a visit to my home from the FBI. Now, you know I nearly passed out when I opened my door and the men in Black flashed their badges and asked for me. Wasn't this stuff only supposed to happen in the movies? Initially, I rolled my eyes and just chuckled to myself, as they already knew who I was. Their purpose was to question me about this same professional. I told them, as I had previously relayed to the AG, I did not have any knowledge of what she did for other providers and provided the FBI with the same documentation I had given the AG.

In January 2017, the AG returned to my office again. The purpose of this meeting was to let me know the outcome of their audit. I still had not received a response from Indiana Medicaid regarding my appeal of the 2012 audit claiming I had owed them $20,000. The AG concluded the issues with my billing were minor. They were more typographical errors, i.e., putting him instead of her, missing a date, but no evidence of fraudulent billing. I was relieved to hear this news. The AG also advised me to develop a corrective action plan and they would be submitting their final report to Indiana Medicaid along with some recommendations. I really wanted to believe the AG, but based on my past experiences, I simply did not trust them.

As I'd mentioned earlier, the Federal Public Defender for the professional accused of fraud, had subpoenaed me as a witness. I wanted to throw this subpoena in the trash but I knew the consequences would not be in my best interest. So I complied and testified. If I thought my anxiety was severe then, nothing could have prepared me for what it would be like upon entering a federal building. I now had feelings of impending doom. The search I endured by security to enter into the building felt like a strip search. If humiliation were a person, it would have been me.

As the year 2017 came to an end, I still did not have a response regarding the status of my case from Indiana Medicaid. I was starting to come to the realization that neither my business nor myself would ever be the same. On top of this, I had lost the passion to continue in the mental health field. Although, I wholeheartedly believed this was my calling in life, I decided to step away in an attempt to reduce my anxiety and put my life back together. I believe that whatever God has called us to do, even if we detour, He will lead us back to it.

In April 2018, I sold my private practice. It was honestly a bittersweet moment for me because it was something I had nurtured from the ground up. I really wasn't sure of what to do next. But I served a God who could do anything but fail. So, with faith and fortitude, I realized I could still help others but not from a mental aspect. I slowly began to rebuild my life and worked out the logistics of starting a new business in the process. In October 2018, I received a certified letter from Indiana Medicaid. The letter was to apprise me that the payment suspension had been lifted. This was great news, but it had come a little too late. I filed the letter away and carried on with my new business adventure.

When this fiasco started, I was afraid to open letters from Indiana Medicaid because they caused my anxiety to flare out of control, but my attitude had started to change. I was now convinced there was nothing else Medicaid could do to hurt me. I had finally taken back control of my life. Beyond the emotional and mental toll, homogeneity, and algorithm biases this ordeal had on my livelihood and mental well-being, I want every Black woman to know that authenticity is integral to your well-being. In the midst of the storm and adversity you must continue to be your authentic self and fight for what you know is right. I hope my story shows someone out there how bias algorithms used by systems are programmed to work against Blacks.

The two other Black women who were also going through Indiana Medicaid audits during the same time were also severely impacted by these biased algorithms. For one of them, the financial losses wreaked havoc on her business and unfortunately, she was forced to close, too. She compared her emotions to that of being on a merry-go-round and at every stop, a new emotion would surface. She stated, "I found myself unable to make day to day decisions in my best interest." She also revealed that if it had not been for her faith, she would not have survived this ordeal. Eventually, she relocated and still practices in the field of social work. The other Black woman suffered financial losses to the point that she had to downsize her agency and deplete her retirement accounts in order to keep her agency open. She also described feelings of helplessness and being treated unfairly by a system that appeared to be controlled by algorithms. She had stated, "It has been through the support of my family, my faith and prayers that I sustained the losses." She secured a two-year governmental contract and has decided that she will close her agency and retire upon its completion.

Although the choices may seem technical and small to the individuals who've made these algorithms, they have had profound impacts on the lives and businesses of Black mental health providers. While human biases can be challenging to quantify or to diminish completely, it is not the case with algorithms.

Black Roadblocks

Dr. Tara Hines-McCoy

AS A HUMAN Resource professional for over fifteen years I have become immune to strong conversations. Yes, they are all different, but their outcome has a recurring theme of behavior or performance issues ultimately leading to separation with the organization. I have worked for fortune 500 companies who fortunately have had great leaders of all races and unfortunately had leaders, specifically for me, Black females, who have not shown care and concern for other Black women. Intentionally or unintentionally, co-signing with white leaders who had limited insight into behaviors or performance of Black females undermines women within their own racial community. I know because this unseen barrier caught me off guard. Throughout my human resources career, I have received promotions, coupled with exceptional to strong performance feedback although, this was never without opportunities to improve as we all have regardless of the industry. For that reason, it has always been clear that I possess the qualities and experiences of a leader. I have displayed leadership by managing a team, being chosen to roll out corporate initiatives, and having experiences from other corporations, however that was not enough for me as a Black female in corporate America. The reality is that perseverance through formal education and corporate training can be threatened by one leader who does not see you as a leader.

The year 2018 proved to be another promotional opportunity in my corporate career but unlike before, this promotion included uprooting my daughter who was a junior in high school from our comfortable and familiar surroundings of fifteen years. The comfort of her grandparents living seven minutes away, tagging along on field trips, preparing daily dinners, unexpectedly dropping off groceries, and always being a phone call away to join other parents, caregivers, and grandparents in the infamous pick up line after school. Yes, their unconditional love and undying support made me shudder to think of moving three hundred miles away and unable to see them daily. As a single Black mother, I thought this move would position both my daughter and I for success. Relocating from Arkansas to Texas would offer unlimited college choices on all levels. My daughter could explore college options and remain close to home, while allowing us to spend more time with my brother and his family, in addition to raising the bar on my career. No, not all those things came to pass, but when things do not work out as planned, I have never been one to wallow in the sand. Instead, in the words of Ariana Grande, I simply say "Thank you, next."

Fortunately, it has never taken me long to study the personalities of people. Their intentions resonate with me within the first few minutes of the conversation. Therefore, I knew the behavior seemed odd when the vice president would go out of his way to say we are at headcount numbers in monthly meetings as a way to reassure the team their jobs were secure and even going so far as to drop by my office only to share the same message. Therefore, I quickly noticed within five months into the position he was no longer stopping by and or stressing that we were at full headcount.

My direct leader (who reported to the VP) was a woman who possessed a strong HR background but really needed an assistant versus a human resources business partner on her team. Our interactions always included her handing off administrative tasks to me and she would insert either before or after the meeting the required question of "Is there something I could help you with?" This question always felt like a second thought. Basically, something for a leader to ask to make them feel like they are showing care and concern, although the meeting was clearly intended to be a session of what I need you to do for me. During the first three to five months, I'd occasionally communicate to my manager that the role was more tactical than I'd thought. Strategy was broached when the administrative tasks were done, but this was rare.

One month short of a year being in my new role, my direct leader, colleagues, and several others were promoted. In addition, two things happened back to back. My leader who was being promoted insisted we have lunch together. Lunch? The first lunch we had since I had started in the role. During the lunch I could tell she had something to say, but in true non-direct fashion, she simply stated as a result of the transformation the organization would be looking for leaders who were strategic. Therefore, honing in on strategy and by the way, being strategic is not something that happens overnight. I understand strategy and made a point to raise the issue that the role was not strategic and somehow this topic had landed in my lap. Next up the VP whom I had very little contact with, met with me to share that they (still not sure who they were) were not seeing the strategic muscle or ability. He stressed we would work through it in the coming months (as if there was some sort of partnership). However, he would be forthcoming with me regarding changes that would impact my role. "What does that mean," I replied. "Nothing for now, but I will definitely keep you in the loop as things change," he responded. At this juncture, not only was I to expect changes to my role, I also needed to redefine the meaning of strategy.

Strategy is in the eye of the beholder. A critical piece of being strategic must be observed by performance. Unfortunately, in this case that had not occurred at least by the VP. Strategy is one of many buzzwords in HR. Once you are labeled with a buzzword, it never goes away regardless of the countless strategies, succession plans, or agility models you implement. In reality, I was strategic in the route I'd taken to work daily. I was strategic in picking out what outfit I was going to wear and where I sat during meetings. I strategically started as an HR Intern and overtime was promoted to a senior HR business partner. The conversation of lacking strategic skills hit me like a head on collision. If both my direct leader and the VP were having a conversation with me about being strategic, who else had they had this conversation with and why? After fifteen years in corporate America, I felt the need to prove my worth. During this time, a Black female was hired into a vacated human resources director position. Initially I was shocked as my former organization had built a reputation for their inability to keep Black females in HR, especially at the director level. Due to the departure of my leader, I would now be reporting to this new director. Once again by studying personalities, I realized it is what it is, and you know what you know during our initial meeting. Yes, she had a seat at the table, but I've realized a seat does not mean a voice, at least not a voice for me.

Instead of coming into the organization as an advocate, she arrived and accepted the narrative that was being described or told by leaders who did not have full visibility to the work I had been doing. I realized if a leader states they are trying to stay under the radar there is no way they can be a champion for me. In January 2020 a younger Black female had arrived with no HR experience and was promoted to the team from a client I was supporting. She'd been given the same title I had, but two compensation grade levels above my grade to keep her whole. Essentially, playing the diversity numbers game. Calibration session had arrived and I had joined her for support during the first session with a new client she now owned and one that I was merely supporting. I can lead calibration sessions in my sleep. In short, HR facilitates the sessions however, the leaders own the dialogue. As a reminder, I supported the team this newly promoted Black female had transferred from, which meant I had also led calibrations for her former team as well.

The calibration was nothing out of the norm because the senior leader for the team was extremely hands on and would run the meetings at his own pace and preference. I chimed in when needed, but I am not one to provide feedback just for the sake of talking. To my surprise, when the VP asked this newly promoted Black female how the calibration session was managed, the feedback she provided was, "She expected me to lean in more." Lean in more? I was there for support, I was never the lead HR for this client, nor did I feel the need to chime in more than what was needed. I had fifteen plus years of HR experience. I clearly knew how to lean in, and lead calibrations but found this session being used as a compass as to how I performed. I was taken aback by the fact that someone who lacked HR experience could only offer negative feedback regarding a process they had little knowledge of.

Fast forward to the annual performance review in February 2020. I'd received a strong rating with overall good comments. The review was short and sweet. What happened afterward is one for the records. After discussing my performance, the director stated, "I'm taking off my HR hat for an off the record conversation." She proceeded to tell me, "Let's discuss what you want to do." To which I replied, "I have a passion for training and development, working on projects similarly to the one I was supporting and would like to progress to a director." She responded by saying she did not see any opportunities becoming available in the areas I wanted to pursue any time soon. She continued to ask if I had been looking outside the company. I replied "No, should I?" She stated, "I would if I were you." I replied, "I would not consider looking outside the organization especially considering that the company had relocated my family." She replied, "If I could take care of the relocation would you consider it?" I stated, "I guess, but that was not something I was actively pursuing." She replied, "Let me ask around and see what I can do." This was described as an off the record conversation, but somehow, I was pretty confident this was a set up from the beginning. I'd slowly began to put the pieces together that it was highly likely my reporting structure was moved to the new Black director as a way to alleviate any potential race or discrimination allegations. Unbeknownst to her, she had participated in conversations about my performance noting areas for development and the information was being absorbed to add to the VP's perspective that I was not strategic. The deck was stacking up quickly.

The thing I look forward to the most is waking up each day to new revelations. The day after our conversation did not disappoint. Upon arrival, the VP was back in the office. In his cool and collective fashion he dropped by my office, leaned into my desk, and stated, "Hey I am not like that. I would not ask you to pay back relocation. Let's discuss timing that makes sense for everyone." I am certain my facial expression clearly communicated I was in complete shock. He then proceeded to the director's office next door to have a conversation. Timing is everything because I had a meeting with the director already scheduled for that day and I intended to address the matter immediately. She ended up joining the conference call in my office and it took all of the professionalism I had to get through the call with little to no eye contact with the enemy that looked like me sitting on the other side of the table.

As soon as the call wrapped up, I referenced our conversation from the day before and prefaced it with, "I thought our discussion was off the record." However, the VP just dropped by my office to reassure me that we could work through timing as if I've requested an early out. The director was extremely apologetic and stated she did not mean for the situation to unravel that way. While seeking direction regarding relocation she felt inclined to mention our conversation to her manager, the VP for our team. Really? Who unintentionally does that? I clearly and eloquently communicated to her that I had shared the feedback based on our private conversation and I did not appreciate her willingness to go and share that information. She continued to apologize and said building trust among her team was really important to her and asked what she could do to regain my trust. I replied with nothing because I did not trust her, and I would address the matter with the VP. This was a small but clear opportunity to build trust while proving our reliability to one another as Black women which unfortunately, had led to distrust. These incidents were two classic examples of Black women who betrayed their race for the greater good of the organization while attempting to leverage their relationship with white leaders or cohorts. In other words, a traitor.

Racism is an interesting creature as it can be presented in such an unobscured manner that it slides right over your head. As you trek along in life, the smallest or biggest milestones and accomplishments somehow take you back to that day and time you were faced with roadblocks. That is when you know for sure that you, too, have come face to face with some form of unacceptance, micro-aggression, racial hostility, double consciousness or colorism. If you are like me, you have told yourself that you are not bothered by these biases. However, together over time, they can create doubt, lack of confidence, and uneasiness for no logical reason besides the fact that, deep down, you are always trying to ensure you are as good or better than the white athlete, student, or colleague.

In the same way we as Black people accuse white Americans of throwing us under the bus, not supporting us in corporate America or any industry, the truth of the matter is we also create and add roadblocks for one another within our own race. To be clear, Black females are not looking for a pass, we are not asking to be held to a lesser standard or asking anyone to look the other way. Rather, we are simply expecting to be held to the same standards as our white counterparts, given real opportunities for development and promotion while also expecting to receive the acknowledgement we deserve for the hard work, endurance, and achievements we have made. In the end, being a Black mother, daughter, and leader in corporate America means having to prove your worth or show you have a strategic arm to be invited to, or to even sit at the table. Black women are being tasked with finding and creating their own development, then being discounted for promotion. This approach will only shift if first, Black women reach back to bring each other along versus creating roadblocks. Second, corporate America changes the trajectory of what diversity and inclusion looks like at the top of an organization. This will ensure diversity is reflected down within the organization to support inclusive practices. Hiring leaders who respect and value the opinions of people who do not look like them, especially women of color is pertinent for change. This will aid in changing the experiences Black females endure in the workplace.

From Darkness to Light

Tyshica R. Lofton, LCSW

I WAS NOT prepared for the racism or discrimination that I would experience while trying to be a change agent in the field of mental health. While Black women are stereotyped as angry, aggressive and hired to meet diversity expectations, because of social conditioning, racism is continually perpetuated in corporate America while downplayed. As a result, Black women tend to go through more unfortunate experiences in the workplace than any other population in America. Thus, Black women are held to a stricter standard on the job compared to their white counterparts even in the field of social work.

In late 2012 I secured a position with an agency and felt so relieved to have a job. Having started the year off rocky, I felt this position would provide steady income for me as I became more established in the field of social work. I had previously been laid off from one position and unexpectedly, the next position I secured was eliminated suddenly. While trying to figure out my next move, I collected unemployment briefly and worked on a clean-up crew removing debris after Hurricane Isaac. A low point in my career, during this time I felt so discouraged and frustrated. Here I was standing in a dumpsite writing tickets for debris removal with a master's degree. So, by the time I secured this new position in the field of social work, the buildup of pressure I had been holding inside was finally released. I could now provide for my family financially. The pay wasn't to my liking and being accessible to clients daily was new to me, but after all I had been through, I was just relieved to have a steady paycheck in my field of study.

My hiring manager assigned me to shadow another coworker, and initially, they seemed nice. The person was from another country and identified as white. She was likely a few years younger than me, although I never asked. Roughly a week into this new position, I was informed by the person I was shadowing that the hiring manager was resigning. In addition to that, the department was being overhauled and there were new scheduling expectations. My white coworkers were a feisty group and made it blatantly clear they didn't agree with the changes in leadership, new expectations, or scheduling accountability. They complained so much that the agency hired an outside company to perform personality assessments and provide team building exercises to assist in accepting or adapting to the changes. Yes, the agency went to great lengths to appease the concerns of my white coworkers, but the Black coworkers were different. We held our heads down, completed our work and minded our business. No, we were not happy about the changes either, but unlike our white colleagues, we didn't speak out. Unfortunately, there was this unspoken energy that Blacks couldn't do what our white counterparts had done in order to not experience an unfavorable outcome.

A few weeks later we met the new manager, and yes it was a white person. That person came in with this "we are the world" and "teamwork makes the dream work" type of speeches and attitude. They seemed authentic, but time would tell the real story. By this time, I had my full caseload and I quickly started to realize something wasn't right. All the clients I had been assigned, seemed to have been recently switched over from another person's caseload or new to the program all together.

The white clients I'd been assigned seemed to have the highest needs in the entire program. Remember earlier I mentioned needing to be accessible on a daily basis for clients? Well these clients took full advantage of that aspect of my position. In addition to being high need mental health clients, they also had not received case management services for a lengthy time period. They proved to be difficult in other areas as well, including scheduling sessions with a personal care attendant (PCA) due to their frequent inappropriate and aggressive behaviors. This quickly became a challenge for me. If I couldn't find a PCA worker, the responsibility fell on me and I was required to work that shift, too. This often included cooking, cleaning, and sometimes bed baths. If that wasn't bad enough, these clients would make emergency calls in the middle of the night, for something that really could have waited until the morning or when I was scheduled to go out to visit them again.

The weight of this job became extremely heavy. I started to feel stressed again. In addition, I was exhausted, alone and depressed. I hated my job, and this dark place that I was now in. I eventually went to the new manager to express my concerns, but honestly, that was a waste of my time as there was not a resolution to bring the number of cases that I had down to a manageable number. I knew the manager had a lot to deal with in addition to the demanding personalities of my white coworkers, the guarded Black workers, and a new employee (me) that had a ton of questions. Nevertheless, I felt dismissed and unsupported in my role.

Over time, I gained more experience regarding the responsibilities of the job in spite of this ongoing dread that I had to go to work daily. In addition to the internal battles that I was fighting, I also started experiencing more conflict with the person I was shadowing. I attempted to address the caseload concerns again and was told it would be addressed at some point, but they had no idea when that would be. The new manager noticed I was a fast learner, independent and resourceful, which didn't sit well with the person I was shadowing. They seemed to feel insecure about the manager taking notice of me. Little did they know, the manager would eventually use all of this to justify me maintaining my heavy caseload.

It was no secret I was advocating for a more equitable caseload, so it seemed the person I was shadowing would talk about me. Soon my coworkers were chiming in saying their clients were difficult, too. I felt my concerns were being negated. The new manager tried to reassure us that we were all on the same playing field and we would all be given the same respect, but I soon discovered that wouldn't be the case.

One morning I awoke for work and I began to cry as I sat on the edge of my bed. I started to question my career choice. I felt so many different feelings and had many negative thoughts. I was truly depressed. I needed the steady income, yet I feared that I was experiencing a breakdown. For once in my life, I didn't know what to do to pull myself out of this funk. A feeling which one could compare to quicksand, the more I tried to fight for myself, the deeper I sunk into a state of depression.

One day, I went into work and after lunch, I was called into the manager's office. When I went in, I was hoping to hear there would be a revamping of the caseloads to help distribute the high demand clients equally across agency workers. To the contrary, I was met with accusations against my character. The manager told me that someone reported they overheard a conversation where I referred to a client in a disrespectful manner and called a client a *nigger*. They went on to say I was also excessively on my cell phone, engaging in personal calls throughout the day. At no point did the manager ask to hear my side of the story, or try to mediate this situation, instead I was verbally reprimanded for these alleged behaviors. Finally, at the end of our meeting, the manager went on to tell me I seemed depressed and that I might want to consider seeing a therapist.

I was in complete shock. The manager believed my coworker, taking everything that they said at face value. No questions were asked of me and not once was I asked anything regarding the accusations. I was now livid, hurt and offended. It felt like a dam had broken inside of me. I told the manager how I felt and asked if they would bring my accuser into the meeting. The manager refused. Realizing the extent of my emotions, they then tried to de-escalate the situation, but I was so angry and offended it took me a few minutes to calm down. I became so overwhelmed I began to cry. Once I broke down emotionally, the manager began to suggest I see a doctor for a prescription for depression medication. It was at that moment I realized I needed to find another job, or I might end up in jail for physically attacking someone. Upon leaving the office, the team was aware of the accusations made and that the manager had addressed them with me. One of my Black coworkers approached me after the meeting and shared that the person I was shadowing was talking about the meeting the manager was having with me. She'd admitted the person I was shadowing had an issue with Blacks and that they were back-stabbers. I knew beyond a shadow of a doubt, it was time to go!

The very act of resigning from that job was like the sun hitting my skin after a cold, dark, rainy day. I felt free, revived and affirmed. Unfortunately, I realized I did not follow-up with HR to file a grievance, explore my rights or request to have a mediation done. I honestly felt it wouldn't have changed anything. I believe I was asked to do an exit interview and while I didn't feel it would make a difference, I was brutally honest before walking out the door.

I didn't realize how much race played a part in the way I was being treated until I left. It was hard to process while I was in the midst of the storm and honestly, I wasn't mentally prepared. I've learned so much about being a Black woman in corporate America from that position. We are truly the most undervalued, mistreated and misunderstood workers in America. My personal lessons: Never stay where you're not wanted, valued, or treated equally. Your education presents you with options. Don't abandon your passion, dreams or desires because others are uncomfortable with the color of your skin.

I now own a private practice providing mental health and support services to those in need. I provide impactful services that lead to the improvement of quality of life. To help others heal and grow is a complete blessing. Since the unveiling of this unfortunate experience, I've been shining bright and I promise you, I won't ever let racism or discrimination dim my light again.

Gracefully Broken:
How Tragedy Became a Testimony

....

Nadeige Pochette

This is a test. The fact that you have chosen to seriously read this book, is an indicator that you are "on the path" to health, wealth and prosperity. You have done the best that you can with what you know, yet you thirst. Jesus replied, "If you only knew the gift God has for you and who you are speaking to, you would ask me, and I would give you living water, "John 4:10 New Living Translation.

This is only a test.

LONG BEFORE I had achieved major accomplishments of any sort, I was a baby girl born to an immigrant family from the Island of Haiti. After being born in Brooklyn, New York, my family relocated to the small village of South Lancaster, Massachusetts where I was raised as a seventh-day Adventist. During my mid-teens my family experienced a difficult divorce and I spent my latter teen years with my mother. I graduated from the University of Massachusetts in Lowell and joined the world of corporate America. I mention some biographical information because much of how we experience life begins with the foundation laid during our primary and formative years. As I take you on my personal journey, my wish is to not only share how I've shifted from being a victim to a victor but to encourage all of those struggling to find the light at the end of the tunnel. Many scriptural references are made from the Bible as a source of spiritual principle and universal law, because that is what I know well. The same spiritual ideas can be found in most other religions.

Growing up, I remember having countless experiences which taught me that my life as a woman of color would not be equal to those of my fairer skinned counterparts. I would be expected to work twice as hard in order to attain the material economic gains that would make life sustainable. Despite the daily rigors of life, my family, church, and community expected me to be resilient and press forward.

I can recall one situation in which I had entered into a contract for a junior level position. I had worked in the industry for about three years before receiving a better title and I was hungry for the next position. The company that hired me was just as hungry as I was, but did not treat its employees that well, which was unknown to me at the time. During my interview, one red flag I'd overlooked was that the supervisor I was being paid to support, did not appear to look too happy at work although she had been working there for more than ten years. She was a white Latina who had dropped out of college. I quickly learned that she was constantly under high pressure to produce while constantly keeping a lookout for possibly being replaced by someone who was better than her. When I came to her rescue, she was relieved to find help, but always watching me to ensure that I did not outperform her. Within one year of working at the company, I had reached a peak level of performance and that was when things changed drastically because the stakeholders of the organization began to recognize me. Instead of encouragement, I was met with resistance. I was now being viewed as a threat. Tougher and unrealistic expectations started to be placed on me and I was monitored for mistakes. My supervisor made it clear that she wanted me to leave because she had been there for a long time and did not want anyone to take her place or be promoted over her in the department.

I worked until I knew it was time to leave. She was thrilled that I was leaving, and she made it apparent. I did not say a word in retaliation. The standard that the enemy had placed on me to work harder, faster and cheaper would be the same standard placed against him (Isaiah 59:19). As a result, God placed me in a better place where my achievements were recognized and appreciated by the world. That supervisor now had to compensate for the loss of losing essential employees. She struggled to do that because she was not a rainmaker in the business and the toxic atmosphere of the company began to circulate. She never found anyone suitable to replace me and eventually sought to hire me back. By that time, I was in a better place and living my life. To make a long story short, the company ended up going out of business and she had to find another place of employment.

As difficult as it was for me to endure this type of environment, I remained in prayer. It was God who had told me when to leave and not to return. Although the relationship with the company could not be salvaged, I had to pray for all of the individuals involved in that business so that God could heal the hearts of those who allowed unethical practices to dry the company out. I believe that God is a good God and He is a God of a "second chance." And even if we never sit at the table in perfect harmony together right now, God will provide another opportunity to make it right.

"Stay in the Lord and he will direct your paths and make them straight. And no matter how evil these days may become, "We know that God causes everything to work together for the good of those who love God and are called according to his purpose for them (Romans 8:28 NLT)."

This was not the first time that I'd gone through a difficult time. My strength came from a teachable moment in my mid-twenties which led me to challenge my understanding of my environment and my place in it. I had been working toward an engineering degree and was experiencing difficulty getting through the program. I was coming to the realization that I might have to take a different course to achieve my overall career goals. After experiencing a deep exhaustion, I became unable to work. I felt isolated in pain and sorrow. My family could not understand why I could not bounce back as I had done in the past. I had reached my breaking point. Now that I was shattered, I could either choose to use the strength that was left to piece myself back together again or remain broken. I chose life! Despite the thrashing, there was just enough hope left to try. Jesus told his disciples, "I tell you the truth, if you had faith even as small as a mustard seed, you could say to this mountain, 'Move from here to there,' and it would move. Nothing would be impossible" (Matthew 17:20 New Living Translation). I never would have imagined that my setback would be a setup for greatness.

When every avenue I'd known did not resolve my dilemma, I did something I had not done in years, I reached for the Bible. There were no more options from which to choose and there was nothing left to lose. I found myself amidst the story of "A House Built Upon a Rock."

Building on a Solid Foundation

24 *"Anyone who listens to my teaching and follows it is wise, like a person who builds a house on solid rock. 25 Though the rain comes in torrents and the floodwaters rise and the winds beat against that house, it won't collapse because it is built on bedrock. 26 But anyone who hears my teaching and doesn't obey it is foolish, like a person who builds a house on sand. 27 When the rains*

and floods come and the winds beat against that house, it will collapse with a mighty crash" (Matthew 7:24-27 New Living Translation).

I suddenly started to feel a wave of self-realization. Perhaps if I had not neglected time with the Lord, I would not have experienced so much inner turmoil. Perhaps I was like that house built on sand. I was pressed on every side and faith in myself and my abilities were no longer enough to support my ambition. I had to learn to trust in something greater than me. Then, instead of focusing on the degree, my prayer became "Lord, please help my disbelief." That prayer was answered with more spiritual books and a family of faith which were important to healing, guidance and allowing the Holy Spirit to renew my thought patterns.

Do Not Love This World 15 Do not love this world nor the things it offers you, for when you love the world, you do not have the love of the Father in you (1 John 2:15 New Living Translation).

When I took the time to examine the thought patterns imposed by society and compared them to spiritual laws and principles it helped me to choose thought patterns that were more loving and beneficial to me and those around me. Thoughts really do become things because your thought-life is the starting point from which actions and behavior truly arise. When right-thinking is in play it is easier to flow in the natural direction that God is leading without unnecessary resistance to His direction. It took time to learn that although society may deem me as less than, the Father deems me as the head and not the tail (Deuteronomy 28:13). Even if a supervisor never could truly understand my value or worth, that was okay. Any opportunity afforded me was given by the Lord and my responsibility was to work like I was working for Him, and He will take care of the rest in His perfect timing. Therefore, the door to opportunity was never really lost in the first place. It only appeared to be lost because I had blurred vision. By peering at the circumstances of life through God's perspective, opportunity is ever present, even when it arrives in a manner that is seen as unfavorable.

The Kingdom of Heaven 33 Seek the Kingdom of God above all else, and live righteously, and he will give you everything you need (Matthew 6:33 New Living Translation).

Looking back, it is interesting how I learned to lean on God only when there was no one else to lean on. God had allowed everything that I've known or was used to, to fall away so that I could know who He really was. Sadly, most people don't discover God until a major fall. Now I can be thankful for the bitter experience because it would have taken me longer to seek His presence if things had worked out differently. Oftentimes, God will allow us to endure a test in order to assess what He can trust you with. The Bible says, "For many are called, but few are chosen" (Matthew 22:14 New Living Translation) Choosing to be Christ-like is no easy task to undertake because it involves self-denial, delayed gratification and sacrifice. It requires a humility that can take on rejection and humiliation when making ethical and moral decisions that are in opposition to others.

Although I am no enlightened master, I take great comfort in knowing that I serve a God that is compassionate enough to chasten me whenever I stumble in error so that I do not fall too far from His straight and narrow path. In finding my lost faith, I also needed to acknowledge that there is a counterforce to God in the universe that works to sabotage anything that would bring light and love to the world (John 10:10). And, even though my desire was to live a good and clean life, this life is enveloped in sin (Ephesians 6:10-12). It would take my full faith empowered by the Holy Spirit to resist any distraction from the enemy. Living in harmony also meant releasing the people, places and things that did not serve me well (Psalm 1:1).

I had to distance myself from the negativity that would hold me back in life. Part of that entailed aligning with people, places and things that had matched my values. Now I know to consider that not only in my personal life but also in business. Today, I make an assessment of whom I partner with long before engaging an offer. I also had to learn the virtue of patience. Oftentimes, we gain a strategy toward an end-goal then plan a date for its attainment. Though having a plan is wonderful, sometimes we forget to make our plans flexible for the unexpected events that occur in life. I learned to be more patient with the attainment of my goals because God really has "perfect timing." He knows just how to solve the circumstance of each event, while preparing you for the task ahead, to elevate you to your highest potential. I had to learn to trust the process. I'd also learned that we cannot truly move forward without the act of forgiveness. I needed time to work on me before dealing with my feelings toward others.

Taking full responsibility for my life and affairs, meant dealing with my challenges instead of being stalled by FEAR (False Evidence Appearing Real). I had to educate myself in the areas where my academic curriculum did not; like knowing how to earn and maintain a career that would lead me to a life of balance for health, wealth and prosperity to occur. To do that, in addition to Bible-study and prayer, I sought out literature, mentors, counselors, spiritual advisors and coaches that could help me make the most appropriate choices. After I'd dealt with my own self, I could deal with my feelings toward the people that passed me over for promotion or other opportunities that interested me. Part of my self-healing meant realizing that those that overlooked me were only there for a time and that God would appoint me at the right time and place for His service. I didn't need to dote over lost opportunities only because God has laws, which meant that if I had worked like I was working for Him, the next opportunity would rise forth for me without strain, effort or force. I know that to be true because God is sovereign, and He keeps His promises. I have never had a day where I was left without food, shelter or clothing. I may not have always had what I desired, but I certainly can thank God for His daily provision. Our Father says, "Look at the birds. They don't plant or harvest or store food in barns, for your heavenly Father feeds them. And aren't you far more valuable to him than they are? Can all your worries add a single moment to your life? And why worry about your clothing? Look at the lilies of the field and how they grow. They don't work or make their clothing, yet Solomon in all his glory was not dressed as beautifully as they are. And if God cares so wonderfully for wildflowers that are here today and thrown into the fire tomorrow, he will certainly care for you. Why do you have so little faith? So, don't worry about these things, saying, 'What will we eat? What will we drink? What will we wear?' These things dominate the thoughts of unbelievers, but your heavenly Father already knows all your needs. Seek the Kingdom of God above all else, and live righteously, and he will give you everything you need. So, don't worry about tomorrow, for tomorrow will bring its own worries. Today's trouble is enough for today (Matthew 6: 26-34)." I learned to live in day-tight compartments and entrust my plans for tomorrow in a creator that truly loves me without condition. A creator that loved me enough to provide, protect and guide my decisions when I allowed Him to be first place in my life.

If I had never experienced a break in my life, I would not have been strong enough to experience a breakthrough. Nothing great in life comes easily. The secret to achieving greatness is having the endurance to overcome adversity despite race, gender, economic background and education. No matter how the circumstances of life play out, the door of opportunity is always present when aligned with universal law and principle. The choice is yours to become bitter or better, to decline or to grow, to fall or rise. You hold the key. This is my testimony! I hope that what I've mentioned here encourages you to be better than yesterday. And, I pray that you'll be ready to pass the test.

To Thy Own Self Be True

Lora J. Jerdine

ELEANOR ROOSEVELT ONCE said, "A woman is like a tea bag–you never know how strong she is until she gets in hot water." Or in this case, until her back is up against a wall. Systemic racism established a precedent and a mindset of privilege and entitlement in white Americans, as well as passed down the mindset to the African American that they are not good enough. We are judged by the way every other Black person is viewed in the eyes of a racist society that was not taught the true history of the African American and the value they brought to this country. The history books never talk about the royalty that existed in the African American culture or the greatness, wisdom and inventions that we are responsible for, yet we are always expected to be at least ten times better, smarter and to work harder before any recognition is bestowed upon us. I first saw my true self when I was standing toe to toe and fighting against prejudice treatments and racist situations.

My first encounter of racism happened during my freshman year at Bowling Green State University. The ratio of whites to Blacks was high. It was disturbing to realize there were white students that had never laid eyes on a Black person except those seen on a television screen. They were not alone, I was dazed too, but

71

for different reasons. I did not expect to have to prove to anyone that I was worthy of respect, but that is exactly what I had to do. I was brought up to accept everyone, as long as they treated me with respect. Unfortunately, there were more than a few times I had to assert myself, when situations arose. The white students grew up feeling privilege based on their color, thinking they had more rights than Black students.

I remember a time during my first month in the dorm. I was walking toward the bathroom to shower and I was told by a white student that I had to wait until the other girls, white girls, were out of the bathroom. Of course, this caused a reaction from me, and I not so kindly advised this student that I was first and they could wait for me. In their mind they had rights to the bathroom, the cafeteria lines, and other amenities on campus. Just walking through campus grounds, I noticed their privilege. The behavior that I witnessed was like unleashing powers. I often found myself walking around on campus with my book bag on my shoulder only moving aside when I saw they would not move. In their minds, the campus grounds belonged to them and I was just an intruder. This is where my rebellion to this racists system began. This experience was both sobering and empowering. The one thing I discovered was that I represented the entire race and the entire race would be judged based on my performance, regardless of whether or not I liked it. "When I am weak, his strength is manifested. During the difficult situations our faith is tested."

My next experience with racism occurred at my first job as a twenty-year old with no degree, but the skills required for the position. Being the youngest sibling and feeling unheard and unseen during my childhood, I instinctively became an overachiever. This became my advantage for such a time as this. I landed my first job at a company that came to be the second largest telecommunications company in the US. I worked in a sales office with fifteen sales reps, six customer service reps, one receptionist, an office manager, a district sales manager, and various others. I covered administrative duties for the office; typing proposals, service documents, ordered office supplies, managed the mailroom and assisted with reporting revenue. My peer in another local office managed the same duties for the adjacent location. Her name was Karen, her and I became good friends. She became very significant to my story.

A circumstance I became too familiar with and had to initially adapt to, was being the only one or the one of two Blacks. At this particular job, there was one other Black male and I at the time. The ratio in this office alone was twenty-four to two, not counting the other local office personnel, there were no Blacks in that office at all. The conversations I would overhear regarding hiring Black salespersons was, "We can't find anyone who is qualified." I remember a time when they finally hired a Black salesman in the other office. I was happy to know I helped to bring that person in.

During my time, it became very annoying that Black employees were expected to mingle and gather with our white peers, but not with each other. Our gatherings made our white peers uncomfortable, and our conversations often resulted in them inquiring about our discussion. In the words of the late, great Marvin Gaye, "What's going on?" The standards for the two groups were noticeably different. Yes, affirmative action forced the hands of businesses to hire Blacks, but there was no plan in place to support diversity and inclusion. I often felt like I had lived in two different worlds and in order to survive, I had to learn to adapt to their white privilege while learning who I was as a Black woman. I had to fight against something I knew, innately shouldn't even exist. The blatant message was as loud as the sound of two cymbals slamming together. Whites are better, smarter and more capable. But I knew better and for them, it was more of "It's not what you know, but who you know."

I was soon indoctrinated into the culture of the corporate

office. It was a competitive environment and the energy was high. It all began when there was a shake up in the sales office, in the telecommunications world, this was not unusual. The two people with all the knowledge of office functions had left the company. The office manager and the sales manager were now gone, which left Karen and I in the other office. Fortunately, we worked together, and figured out the systems that helped the office to run smoothly and together, we implemented new procedures and processes. We also managed the administrative duties for both offices as a team. Interestingly, we complimented each other well and eventually developed a great friendship where we shared precious life moments raising our children. She was and still is, my sister from another mister.

After my first year, my annual performance review was due. Considering we did not have steady management for half of that time, I was a little concerned. Who would provide my performance review, and would I get a much-deserved pay increase? I was an overachiever, if I received a "B" in class that was not good enough, I had to have that "A." My review ended up being administered by a new manager who had been hired three months prior. The gossip in the office was she was hired because of her husband's relationship with the senior manager, and yes; she was white. As to what happened next, well, in one word, displeasure. I had received an unsatisfactory rating on my annual performance review. I felt deflated, devastated, and hurt just to name a few of my emotions before I became angry. My hard work and dedication had been completely overlooked. The new manager was very fond of Karen and she blatantly gave her credit for what *we've* accomplished; as if I was not there working my behind off. I was angry and the hint of defeat tried to settle in, but I had used my anger to motivate me in seeking a solution.

According to the company's HR policies, an employee's only repercussion when in disagreement with a performance review is to decline signing the document. That was not enough for me, I could not just accept the unfair rating and wait another year to get a raise. I felt a sense of entitlement and that my work should have spoken for itself, but instead it went unnoticed. One of the behaviors I'd noticed and still see is, it's easier to accept and relate to someone that looks like you. How were Blacks expected to have a level playing field? I did not want to be pacified by merely not signing the document. I needed them to acknowledge their mistake and correct my performance review.

What I did next was the beginning of an exercise I like to call "gaining my respect" and providing the receipts. I conducted a poll from all the sales and service reps in the office that I'd performed work for. They were more than willing to speak up for me. On a positive note, I'd developed wonderful relationships with some of them. Each of these individuals wrote a letter of recommendation and provided accolades for the work I had done. I then drafted my own letter identifying my accomplishments and gave examples of jobs that I had performed. I had at least twenty letters as well as my own. My written rebuttal was three pages long and I had submitted it along with the letters from my colleagues and peers. Professional tip: never feel like you have to agree or accept someone's misinterpretation of you. My name was being discussed behind closed doors. "Stand for something or you will fall for anything." I had to stand up and be heard. My rebuttal received the attention that I needed in order to make a difference. There was a sense of disbelief that I had gone to the extent that I did. As I stated earlier in the story, they only expected me to disagree by not signing the document. Let the record show, I disagree, "Crap!" What was that going to do? My spirit led me to stand up and fight or sit down and allow them to step all over me, leaving me to feel like I am not as good as any one of my white peers. Upper management ultimately requested another performance review in three months, and I was given a

10% pay increase. When I had left the corporate world at the end of 2016, I was lucky to have received a 1% increase.

After thirty-two years in corporate America, I've discovered a few things. First, respect is earned not by keeping quiet but by standing up and speaking out. Second, always be on top of your game. Be aware of your every move and the moves of those around you. Strive to be the best in whatever position you are in. Third, never stop documenting. It was during this season of my life that I learned the value of documentation. I made sure to document every conversation, day to day activities and every encounter no matter how big or small it may have been. Being the only Black person in a corporation should not be common in 2020, but here we are. I don't think those outside of the Black race understand the challenges and difficulties we face by being the only colored face in the room. The experience is more difficult because of the fact that we are aware that we are seen as a representative for the entire race, which honestly, isn't fair. The day to day scrutiny that one must endure by being the only Black in an organization becomes an additional pressure that we as Blacks must bear, especially Black women. Yet, we are constantly labeled as being angry, when in reality we are frustrated and tired of being overlooked, undervalued and left behind. We are ready for change to occur now more than ever in corporate America when it comes to Black women.

Conquering Corporate America: *A Black Girl's Dream and Nightmare*

Stacey Calhoun

RACISM CAN BE hard to identify sometimes; it can literally be happening right before your eyes and still be easily missed until it's too late. When you're working hard and minding your own business you don't always notice the plans that are being plotted against you. You don't realize how your character is being assassinated. You're so in tune with your goals, being the friendly and reliable girl on the team while keeping your head down and not making waves so you fail to protect yourself from the traps.

I remember so vividly when I attended a historical Black college (HBCU), my professor told me during my final project before graduation that I should pursue my postgraduate degree with a focus in marketing. My major was business administration with a concentration in management. She encouraged me to do a focus study in marketing because I'd shared with her I wanted to flourish within that field. She said to me with her deep New Orleans accent, "You need to pursue a postgraduate degree in marketing because it would set you apart from the rest; it's a rare focus degree for African American women." She knew what she was talking about because as an African American woman working within the marketing field, I have endured so many attacks strictly based on who I am as a Black woman and never in regard to my performance. I've been called an overachiever many times by leaders, so I know that my performance has never suffered in any role I have upheld. I've been disappointed by so many acts of racism and sexism throughout my career. It's disappointing how simple ignorance of others can diffuse a flame that is shining so bright all while minding your own business.

I worked in a white male dominant industry, but believe it or not, I was never discriminated against by white males. As a matter of fact, most of my career success all took place under white male leadership. It was always Black and white older women who were found to have unexplainable problems with me. Yes, you read that right, we discriminate against each other especially in the corporate arena. I found myself working and growing quickly within this white male dominant industry where I'd eventually serve as a marketer for over seventeen years. In addition to great highs, I've also experienced some devastating lows during this time period. During the earlier years of my career my most harsh disappointments had taken place in a role that I had eventually held for ten years where I'd given my all to learn and succeed. I came into this industry young and excited; like a sponge, I was ready to absorb anything I could that would make me better. Although I was full of hope, my esteem was challenged often, as defeat was upon me. However, I was prepared to overcome it because I knew I could outperform anyone on the team. My dedication was different. I took pride in hitting consistent homeruns and exceeding goals. This was my pay back in a sense to myself for all of my previous failures in life. This was my way to prove to myself that I was worthy and could succeed in the roles I had been given. Things had been great for me up until they weren't. Some things you just don't see coming. How could I continue to be creative, excel and be a comparable leader while enduring the pains I had to silently endure? I was silenced, until being silent was no longer an option…

I was young when I'd started my career within this magical industry, I had accepted a position in finance just to get my foot in the door. As soon as I was eligible, I moved into Human Resources earning a Production Assistant position for the Internal Communication Department. This is where my amateur event skills begin to develop as a professional. I planned internal events for employees, wrote the employee newsletters and oversaw the employee recognition program. I held that position for one full year before getting my break into marketing. I had volunteered for every marketing event I could assist with before getting my shot and it was starting to pay off. I'd worked New Year's Eve slaving and running from one end of the building to the other while stocking stations with party favors. Those heels weren't going to hold me back because I had a goal in view. And not to mention I absolutely go into a zone when I'm in my element of producing events. I was so tired after leaving work that day and all the time I'd spent there was unpaid. It was another volunteer gig, but it would all pay off eventually, I just knew it!

The next week I was offered a job in marketing as an ambassador. It was a bit of a grit and grime position, but I didn't care as long as it was another step in the right direction. I was proud as well as honored to finally make my way into the marketing department in such a short period of time. In this new ambassador position, I basically assisted guests, supplied them with what they needed and attended to other assigned duties. Remember, I told you, it was a grit and grime position, but you couldn't tell me anything. I was willing to haul the trash out if I needed to, that was how bad I wanted to be in marketing. I was faithful to that role for a short four-week stint! *Yes*, four weeks and then God intervened. The position was phased out and I was promoted in four weeks to special events coordinator. I'd thought,

"Oh my God. This was it, I was on my way." I had gone from making $10 an hour to a salary of $30,000 a year and a cell phone at twenty-four years old. What? Oh yes honey, I was given a company phone and business cards. I didn't know where my smile started or ended, it all just seemed to run together. This was a big deal for me coming from a family where my grandparents had worked so hard and tirelessly in the small town plants, and my mother who had raised my brother and me as a single parent while working at the neighborhood pharmacy. During this time my dad and I were estranged, so I didn't know much about his skill set to build from, but I was aware he was a cross country truck driver. So, making this transition into this position where I worked closely with executive leaders, celebrities and planned high-end VIP events for clients was major for me. I was a young single parent who had escaped an abusive marriage trying to find my way in this new environment that wasn't familiar to me by any stretch of my imagination.

During the late 90's it was a rarity to see many African American women in the marketing department. You'd mostly see white males, Black males, or beautiful young white women; not a thick Black girl like myself. But I didn't allow that to deter me, and I continued to navigate the marketing world. This included learning how not to be too Black versus learning the components of a job; if that makes any sense. I was fearful every day that I wouldn't succeed. I had failed at so many other things that this new leap caused major anxiety for me. I was often the voice people heard throughout the business. I was intimidated to be on the microphone. Everyone would always say I sounded so refreshing and very inviting, but I didn't know how to receive those compliments. One reason I struggled in that area was because when I was about twenty years old, I 'd worked for a logistics company and we had a new general manager who was a loudmouth Italian woman from New Jersey. Not to say all Italians are loudmouths, but she in fact was. I digress! She absolutely hated my slow southern drawl. She would ask if I could speak faster and me being naive to her abuse, I'd simply say, "I'll try" and I honestly did. I tried speaking faster when talking to her. I tried changing my tone hoping it was softer and more engaging, but no matter how hard I tried, my voice irritated her to no end. Do you want to know how bad my voice irritated her? One day I came in to work for a meeting about me. Yes, you guessed it, I was terminated and her reason being; she could no longer tolerate my voice and had endured it long enough. Yes, I was fired because of my voice and this shattered me. Although I was broken and felt defeated, I pulled myself out of that embarrassment and found my niche in a whole new industry, one where my voice was appreciated. Guests needed to hear this soft sultry voice on those late nights, Fridays and Saturdays while losing all of their money!

After about five years of working on this magical boat, we were sold, and I was moved to one of our sister properties to the advertising department. In this position I had discovered that I was a well-rounded marketer. I had a creative eye with attention to detail. I was killing the game and flushing out some amazing campaigns. The excitement was short lived as the whole executive team walked out and left the company. Luckily enough my direct report saw my drive and offered me a position at the new property which allowed me to combine my skill set of an event planner and advertising coordinator, giving me a specialist position. This was a supervisory position which gave me a lot of room to have creative control and become the ultimate pitch queen.

But as time went on, everything was good, until it wasn't. This was my first-time reporting to two different people for one role. One manager adored me and gave me full authority to be a creative marketer, while the other manager felt a need to compete with me. This was a new experience for me: I'd never dealt with a leader trying to be my competition. Up until this point, I'd had leaders who would coach and develop me for the next steps in my career. All of them were white. Where my marketing journey had been super amazing for approximately six years it was now coming to a screeching halt. While I started to see a counselor, there was no clear mention of what I was doing wrong at work. I was moved out of my office into a cubical, no longer allowed to be the lead on projects and I was silenced in meetings. I constantly asked myself, "What is really going on?"

Some of these women were new to me. I'd only known one or two people on the team and that was the manager that brought me on board and one other manager. I felt that sense of defeat again that I felt years ago, but this time I was wiser and knew I didn't have to allow any form of abuse to happen to me. I played nice and decreased my visibility because anything I had attempted to do would rub this lady the wrong way. "Out of sight, out of mind, right?" Well I was wrong. Every day I continued to be blamed for something that had nothing to do with me. I was assigned grimy tasks and barred from attending any event meetings. My mean manager, Gretchen, had taken full control. I was the youngest Black girl on the marketing team, and I was thriving in this role, pitching new ideas, executing new events, training event staff and bringing in revenue. I just knew this was a good thing. But somehow, she managed to diminish all the good I was doing, and I suffered in this living hell for six long months.

One night as we were leaving work, I asked her how long she had been doing events. She answered, "This is my first shot at it." I made a quick mental note like "Oh, I see." She continued to talk, "I'd wasted my time being an Executive Assistant all these years and now I'm old and starting over, but I love it." I was so grateful for that conversation because it gave me insight on how to move going forward. I was unaware she had been the only old woman on the team who felt she'd missed opportunities in her career and wasn't happy to see this young Black girl waltzing around all footloose and fancy free, planning stuff while bringing fun to the scene. Nope, I had two "Karens" to deal with at the same time and honey they wore me out. I finally visited Human Resources to discuss my situation and get advice on how to handle the harassment I was enduring. What I didn't know was that the Team Relations Manager wasn't on my side. Everything I'd discussed with her, was shared with my manager. Now I was left exposed with no covering to protect myself from the upcoming firestorm.

Shortly thereafter, I was called into Gretchen's office with the Human Resource Director present. My mind immediately went back to the day I was terminated in my early twenties. I was asked to sit down, so I did and was immediately prompted to not say a word. The HR Director started the meeting by reading off the complaints I had shared with the Team Relations Manager (did I mention this was a Black woman) and asked me if this had been my conversation with her. I said no. The conversation she read back to me wasn't the same one I'd had with the Team Relations Manager. She had added so many things to my original complaint that were not relevant to the situation nor were they true statements made by me. I never said half of what she reported and most of it was personal rumors that were floating around. I was nervous, mad as hell, and scared that I was about to lose my job behind a bunch of jealous women. My manager took over the conversation and literally started shouting at me. She became so upset that at one point in the meeting she started slapping the desk as she yelled. I was blown away. I couldn't believe this was happening and that it was happening to me! This was horrible. I had never experienced a leader shouting at me. As I listened, I pressed my back into the chair I was sitting in, still startled in disbelief. I wanted to punch her in her face. That's how mad I was. To make matters worse, her shouting got louder and louder, "I don't think you are deserving of your pay, and I have put in a request for your pay to be decreased!" Before I could say a word, the HR Director jumped in and told her "Enough, you have gone too far." By this time, I was fighting back tears. All I could think about were my babies and how badly I needed my job. I started to think about how I had put so much effort into myself over the years and overcome my fears. I had worked hard to achieve my goal of being a great marketer. Suddenly everything got fuzzy.

As the HR Director abruptly ended the meeting and sent me home for the rest of the day, I walked out of that office filled with rage, but also with fear of losing my job. My other colleagues who were all middle-aged white women, looked at me speechless not knowing what to say. Everyone had heard the conversation. The other manager I reported to was completely frozen and uncertain how to come to my defense at that moment. I left that day knowing when I returned it would be to pick up my final paycheck.

All of this took place on a Friday, so I had an entire weekend to soak it all in. I went home and took a nap, exhausted from the trauma. I just needed a moment of relief. When I awoke, I picked up my children so we could go to the movies. While at the movies, the other manager called me to apologize for what had taken place earlier that day. She apologized that she was put in a position where she couldn't help me. She too had been isolated. I told her I was fine and wanted to enjoy the night. I'd come up with a plan by Monday. I really didn't want to think about it any longer, I'd had enough. She was crying and said, "No, they want you to come back, and you no longer have to report to Gretchen." I was shocked because I was sure I had been ter-minated, but just like the Bible says, there's always a ram in the bush. What I didn't know was that some of the other managers, one of them being a Black female manager, had spoken up on my behalf. Many of the managers came to my defense even though I had never held a direct conversation with them; nothing more than a hello or a communication pertaining to an event. I was grateful for their input.

My battle with Gretchen came to an end only because I stayed out of her way. Over time, she and I developed a great working relationship, but I never let my guard down with her, ever! As for the other elderly woman, she battled with me for many years after that, but as I grew professionally and matured, I learned how to ignore her hidden racism, too. It wasn't that either of them was jealous of me or that I was so amazing, it was simply that they both were struggling with their own defeat and had issues with me excelling so quickly over the years. I was often called "kiddo" and most times referenced in comparison to their daughters as far as career positioning was concerned. Both of their daughters were close to my age and had not found a path for their careers. In my opinion this, too, was one of the oppositions that concocted against me in their heads. Neither of them took into consideration how hard I had worked to gain the marketing experience that I had. They didn't understand how I had worked with no pay, volunteering my time just to get my foot in the door of this industry. Several times, I was overlooked because, "I just wasn't what they were looking for," and often I'd train people for the very positions I wanted for myself. I earned my spot on that team, but in their eyes, I was simply a Black woman stopping them from achieving their own goals and they weren't having it.

Racism and sexism can be masked and hidden in jealousy, hatred, and flat out meanness. It's a daily struggle for Black women in corporate America. We are judged by our white coun-terparts as well as Black men and sometimes even other Black women. The anxiety that Black women encounter in trying to make sure we're dressed appropriately, our natural hair is well groomed, our nails are properly done, our make-up is nice, our smile is approachable, our tone is not intimidating. These are just a few of the boxes we have to check before even leaving the house to head to work each day. Now let's talk about when we arrive there. We must be perfect to even be considered a valued player on the team. During my tenure within this magical industry, I've had a lot of success and achieved so much, but I had to go through the hazing before I could even gain the opportunity to just be me. It's sad that we've become immune to the abuse and learn how to push through it. I still carry those experiences with me everywhere I go. They are a constant reminder of just how far I have come and how someone can work next to you daily and secretly hate you for no reason at all.

My advice to all women reading my story is that if you are experiencing any form of abuse speak out about it, please don't hold it in. Not speaking out will make you miserable and will ultimately destroy you. If you are at a job that you love and someone is making it hard for you, don't walk away. Use your voice and make some noise! Don't be bullied nor silenced. Learn all that you can and when the time permits, position yourself to leave, coming out better than how you came in. There will be haters everywhere you go, but remember their hate is a testament to what they think of themselves and has nothing to do with you. Stay strong on your journey. Enjoy it as much as you can and keep pushing through like the superstar you are!!!

A Word From The Experts

Managing Job Loss and Race-Related Stress
·················

Carole Sandy, MEd, MSc.(A), R.S.W

BLACK PEOPLE FACE an enormous amount of race-related stressors (visible and invisible micro-aggressions), that contribute to a heightened state of hypervigilance often making the work environment both unsafe and unsettling. Coupled with the fears and concerns of losing one's job, these occurrences usually lead to negative mental health consequences that are often difficult to navigate alone. For this discussion, job loss is defined as "any type of involuntary unemployment which may involve an individual being fired, laid off due to mass reduction in force or pressured into involuntary quitting" (Horn, Mitchell, Lee & Griffeth, 2012).

Over the years in my private practice, individuals have shared how these experiences have impacted their self-esteem leaving them anxious, negative and unable to plan for the future. Meet Marcia, a Black, thirty-two-year old female who recently was laid off from her corporate job. Marcia reported that, when she encountered her peers in the hallway after finding out she was being laid off, it reminded her of the countless times she was questioned about her capabilities as a leader by white males in her office who often undermined her decisions and authority. She recalled the times she was not hired after applying more than once for a certain position and the number of hours and dedication she had given to the organization; she became numb almost like she was no longer in her body. When I met with Marcia, she was still extremely overwhelmed, isolating herself at home and sleeping all day after getting her children to school. She reported becoming easily angered toward close friends and experiencing shame following her job loss. She connected with me after several months, wanting help to deal with her sadness, worry and anger.

When connecting with individuals who have recently lost their jobs here are two issues that often come up: their inner battle concerning how they are supposed to feel about the loss and how much time they may need to reflect upon what just occurred. This is an individual journey, but what I have found is that those who do well with job loss recovery are usually successful because they can concentrate on what is most significant to them while acknowledging the feelings they are experiencing. As a mental health therapist and career coach, I understand that this can be difficult, especially when racial trauma is involved. I can identify with the struggle of making sense of your feelings at a time when most people want to avoid the discomfort and quickly find another job. This decision, if executed too quickly, is often a temporary fix that can work for some individuals, while others, find themselves upset, unfulfilled, and still angry with their previous employer.

Losing a job can be difficult, but when you couple that with the fears and concerns of racial stress for those who are unemployed, they are often more prone to mental health disorders compared to those who are employed, experiencing higher levels of stress, depression and low self-esteem just to name a few. You need support when you lose your job, because unemployment can be a lonely place especially when racial trauma is an ongoing narrative.

Managing our Responses to Job Loss and Race-Related Stress

When our bodies, minds and lives feel violated and our skills feel inferior we need to seek communal support, therapy and a place of refuge (that might mean a conversation with a trusted friend or seeking out the support of a mental health therapist).

Stop, think, listen and receive the gift of acceptance. It is important that we take a moment to breathe, reflect, and listen to what a close ancestor would tell us in this moment and receive the gift of acceptance which is often denied by those in power.

Find ways to get involved in helpful and meaningful tasks that will support the transition at a time that is appropriate for you.

Discover the identity that is authentic to who you are by creating a helpful and diverse narrative by finding work that most reflects how you would like to be seen in the workplace. When we focus on the ego, we get caught up in the stories that are forceful and idealistic.

There are many ways to design your next steps. Work on your self-awareness and self-love which is integral to healing. Be okay with the fear, anger, and frustration. Know that over time you will begin to understand the lessons you were supposed to learn from your previous employer, and what you are not going to tolerate in your life moving forward when it comes to your career. Find ways to verbalize your pain and do not ignore or avoid the emotions that are present.

By creating a more supportive therapeutic recovery plan that focuses on increasing self-awareness and structured personal goals we take into consideration internal and external factors of racial trauma that impact our progress. This work requires that we focus on self-regulatory strategies that address institutional racism so that we can interfere with the thoughts and stories that have tried to silence us and experiences that trigger unhelpful thoughts and feelings.

Carole Sandy is a multi-faceted clinical therapist who works with individuals, couples, and families. Through her various counselling services, she assists people in breaking generational hurts by encouraging them to discover their strengths. Founder of Generation Gap and From Invisible to Visible Therapy, she is dedicated to celebrating the voices and contributions of visible minorities to advance therapy solutions.

Know Your Place

Tracy Daniel-Hardy, Ph.D.

SOME THINGS YOU just can't forget. I remember how I'd felt confused, hurt, embarrassed, and angry. I even remember wearing a sky-blue cotton skirt suit, white blouse, red sandals with a modest heel and red accessories. Unfortunately, I even remember where I sat during the meeting and how quietly most of my colleagues sat throughout the exchange.

He, one of the observers of the exchange, told me I should not have said anything because Mr. Dickens doesn't like being challenged. He told me this as if he was offering me sound advice. Although my movement may not have happened as drastically as it felt, I whipped my head around and said. "So, I should have just let him be wrong?" He looked at me as if he either made a mistake offering me his unsolicited advice or if he was processing what I'd said. He then quickly changed the subject to the business at hand–preparing ourselves for the presentation of scholarship awards. You see, it was senior awards night, and we both had presentations to make. I quietly sat in the second row awaiting my turn on the program while he had requested to go first because he had other things to do, which seemed to be the case every year I'd attended. The reality, in my opinion, was his

91

white privileged, state-of-being refused to allow him to sit and wait his turn like the rest of us.

I'm not sure how I was pulled into the conversation; it's my guess that there had been a meeting before the meeting to discuss how to bring up the topic in front of everyone and how to bring me into it. I'd been around long enough to know that was how many "big" conversations informally made it on the agenda for our regular meetings.

It was a beautiful spring day in May. It was also graduation season. The excitement was in the air. The seniors were excited that the hard work they had done was paying off. They even offered gratitude to anyone who had a role in their journey. I was excited to present several scholarships to graduating seniors from the high school, which happened to be my alma mater, on behalf of the local alumni chapter and my sorority. I was also excited that the meeting would be brief because of all the graduation activities.

Mid-way through the meeting, I was struck by surprise. The meeting seemed to take a detour. It was not going to be what most of us had hoped for. It was going to last much longer, and it would be heated.

A colleague, Susan, was very frustrated about a state department mandate of a digital process that was traditionally a paper process. Apparently, this colleague, a white female, had the ear of Mr. Dickens unlike anyone else. She could implement new concepts that others were barred from even discussing. She was one of the few protected and privileged in our organization. Mr. Dickens protected her and allowed her the privilege of getting away with things that others were chastised for just for mentioning. Private conversations between members of leadership included warnings to newcomers to be cautious in their interactions with her and her assistant, and to avoid crossing Mr. Dickens. Dr. Gates, a Black woman who was Susan's superior, hurtfully included a personal story with her warning to me which included Mr. Dickens unleashing his threatening fury on her because she had disagreed with Susan.

Mr. Dickens and Susan were annoyed with the new state department mandate for online testing. With the previous paper process, all the requirements could be accomplished in a shorter timeframe than it would take for the online process. Mr. Dickens wanted to know why I opposed my colleague's plan and why the state department required that the high stakes process be converted to a digital one. (It was part of my responsibilities to approve, or not, plans such as this for our organization because the plan would be impacted by the organization's network infrastructure). He wanted to know the benefit of having tools available if they could not be used simultaneously to complete the process.

After giving an example of the congestion on the highway during a hurricane evacuation and the example of the bottleneck that would occur if we all tried to exit the door at the same time, he grew furious. The cool spring day started to feel like August in Mississippi–extremely hot and uncomfortable. His furor began to blaze. He began to make that hissing sound he makes when attempting to control his escalating anger. His love-hate relationship with digital processes began to rear its head again. Technology was not making life easier, and Susan was upset and disappointed that her plan could not be implemented without great risk. Initiating high stakes testing of her 400+ students simultaneously on the first day of the state-wide testing window, using an online platform that was not known for reliability, was risky and could be considered gambling with children's academic futures. This was not a good idea.

I was confused and flabbergasted by his response to everything I had said as I tried to explain the problem with her plan. I presented many of the variables that were out of my control and reach, those things that caused issues before that neither I, nor any other director like me, could control. He seemed to be hell-bent on proving a point to her by belittling me in front of the entire team. "You and this technology!" he shouted. For some reason, I don't remember all that he said, but I remember the burn of his accusations. I remember being dumbfounded because Mr. Dickens understood that I was not making the mandate but blamed me for Susan's frenzy. What he had said made very little sense, was very inaccurate, and was not technologically sound. He believed that her plan should work as long as she had enough devices. He was protecting her from the now, outspoken Black female who obviously did not listen to the cautionary tales about treading lightly with Susan.

Although there was not an empty seat in the room, it felt like it. The room was very quiet as if everyone was watching an intense tennis match. It was me against him with encouragement from her. Not just his words, but the force that spewed those words out at me burned—they burned like hell. The tears began to fall. The more I tried to control them, the harder they fell. I don't know why, but I remember the demeanor of the best dressed man in the room. He sat quietly with his head down while slightly glancing at me as if he wanted to rescue me but knowing that it was a dangerous move to make at that moment. The two of them, Susan and Mr. Dickens, seemed pleased with themselves. The others just sat quietly as if they hadn't seen or heard anything. He'd proved his point by protecting her from me and publicly making sure that I knew my place. You see, he'd told me once to remind my Black team member of "her place" with regard to a communication she'd had with Susan.

After being told that I should have been quiet by the privileged observer, I wondered why I didn't just shut up. I'm still not sure why I didn't. I guess I was just tired of being quiet and tired of accepting what I didn't agree with and pretending that it was fine. In this case, I was concerned with ensuring an optimal testing environment for the students while they were focused on convenience and adults. I was, in fact, doing my job.

This exchange was only the beginning. I was fine as long as I complied and responded correctly to the chosen ones, those whose voices mattered more than any other. Those who were privileged to be white (and female, in most cases).

Summers in Mississippi can be brutal; summers in Mississippi are hot and humid. This particular summer, a couple of months after the previous exchange, was brutally hot from the heat of the sun and from the heat of Mr. Dickens. He'd called a meeting that didn't go anything like he'd planned or expected. He'd reassigned duties from our team to an employee who lacked the capacity to do the job and was known for passing duties off to others. There was no prepared agenda and no plan for the meeting even though I'd called prior to the meeting to offer my assistance.

The employee did not accept the assistance. Mr. Dickens began to run the meeting off the cuff when he realized that the employee was not prepared and began making demands and requirements that conflicted with his previous requests for this project. My team and I sat in the back to support the efforts even though the duties were reassigned from our department to the new person. The meeting left many confused and looking to my team and I for explanations and assistance with the new demands.

He noticed the quiet, confused looks and the exchanges many in the audience made and exclaimed, "I see everyone is looking at me like I'm crazy!" I, then, encouraged those who seemed to have questions or comments to say them. With some coaxing, some began to express their confusion. He, then, began a slow, awkward exit from the meeting.

Shortly afterwards, he called me to discuss the meeting and began to unleash his anger on me. He must have held back during the initial exchange on that cool, spring day because this full-blown attack was shocking.

He yelled, "You wanted the meeting to fail!" I yelled back, "I don't *want anything* in this district to fail!" I couldn't stop talking. I had a lot to say that I'd been holding in. He was accusing me of sabotage, and I was offended. My integrity was challenged. We continued to share disappointments with each other until we got tired. He calmed down, so I thought, and we came to an agreement. We agreed to communicate differently and more often. However, I saw and felt the wrath and vindictiveness for years after this phone conversation.

I noticed that the wrath and vindictiveness only seemed to happen to vocal women of color. Many of those women were either pushed out of the organization or left because he (and the others he solicited to join him) made their stay very uncomfortable.

He tried to make my life very uncomfortable. It was blatant in the denial of my travel request. For the first *time ever* in my career, my travel request for professional development was denied. I replied to the denial with an explanation of the purpose of the travel along with a reminder of the professional development requirement because I was certain that the denial was a mistake. It was ignored. My next travel request was questioned and was approved only because the registration had already been paid (prior to putting the finance office on notice to deny all my requests).

I continued to question my travel request denials. In response, he began to announce in meetings that he was limiting travel for everyone except teachers even though groups of other non-teachers, administrators, instructional coaches, etc. were still traveling to conferences and continued to travel throughout that year.

He began to visit our building more often and at varying times of the day. On one occasion, he came just to watch us work and interact with one another without talking to my staff or I. During a subsequent visit after I'd left for an afternoon appointment, he talked to four members of my staff about a student data process.

He called the next day to inform me that he'd visited my department and "Not a fucking soul was there." I remember standing, facing my armoire holding the phone when my jaw dropped just as the temperature had on this fall day. I gasped at his use of the "F" word toward me. I was so stunned that I couldn't form words. I wanted to express that I knew he was lying because my staff had already informed me of his visit.

I'd heard stories about the horrid things he'd said about Black women and the horrible things that he'd done over the years to women of color. I thought it was a coincidence that those things happened to Black women and that the stories were a little exaggerated because surely, he could not do those things so blatantly and stay in a leadership position. The pattern became clear to me and others of the same hue, as long as the Black woman was compliant and didn't challenge him or one of his protected and privileged ones, she was tolerated. I guess we, Black women, have to "know our place."

Credentials and Credibility: How Good Enough is Good Enough

Alyssa Tamboura

MY GRANDMOTHER HAD always told me that I need to work twice as hard for the same opportunities that non-Black folks are freely given. I used to brush her off – I believed in meritocracy. If I worked hard and proved my worth, then others would recognize my value and reward me with the opportunities I sought.

Of course, I had experienced racism as a child in school. Kids hurled racial slurs at me, asked to touch my hair and questioned my intellectual capacities. Other students, all of whom were white, often excluded me from social circles, activities and projects. Yet, my teachers often praised my work. So, when my grandmother harshly told me to get used to the racism from other kids, I naively believed adults wouldn't exclude me as I got older. I thought my work would speak for itself and outshine the color of my skin. It took me years to learn that my grandmother was right. As a Black woman, my credibility and capacities would always be questioned.

A few years ago, I worked as an administrative associate to an executive at a widely known and respected university in the Bay Area. In an office of about twenty people, I was the only

Black woman and only person of color. Every week, our office held a meeting that drew in about twenty or more people from other departments. In this greater collective, I was again the only Black woman and only person of color. Frequently when topics connected to race came up in meetings, people glanced at me to see my reaction. I desperately tried to convince myself that no one saw me as an "other."

Over time, though, the evidence piled up that I was being treated differently. For example, every morning I would pick up newspapers for my boss. Some people started referring to me as "the paper girl." I asked around and learned that the white man who'd held my position before me had never been called "the paperboy."

I felt singled out. Because of my skin color and my role, some of my colleagues viewed me as less than. I thought I could change their minds if I maintained a positive attitude and didn't express the pain I felt. Despite my hard work and contributions though, it was made clear to me that I still had the least amount of privilege of anyone in my office or the greater team.

I was also the only person who was not allowed to work from home – everyone else had at least one day of telecommuting. I was the only person who was paid hourly – despite the fact that my pay was similar to others. I was the only person who did not have their cell phone bill paid for by the office – yet I was still expected to use my personal phone to answer calls, even on my lunch break. Although I recognized my position, I still believed if I worked hard, exceeded expectations in my job duties, and most importantly, did not highlight the inequities, I would eventually be granted the same privileges that everyone else had. I longed for respect.

I was asked to take on a new task: preparing the daily report which was sent university wide, detailing the work of our office and noteworthy accomplishments of researchers at the university. I'd eagerly accepted. This was to be my chance to prove my worth.

After months of writing these reports, I was praised by my colleagues. My writing capacities proved to be more than adequate. It seemed like a good time to ask for more responsibility, such as writing posts for our public facing online blog. The manager for the online publications asked me to draft a sample blog post and pitch it. I immediately dove into the work. I researched a compelling story, interviewed people, and wrote a draft.

To my surprise and disappointment, my blog post was rejected. It was then I learned it had to be approved by the deputy director. She said I couldn't write for the blog because I didn't have a college degree. She didn't reject my piece on its merits, but on grounds that meant I shouldn't even try again. The deputy director gave me a new assignment, one perhaps more suited to my perceived station. I would be transcribing interviews for other writers in the office – a tedious task that was usually contracted out. Ever the optimist, I still thought perhaps this would be a chance to prove my worth, that I could pitch another story in the future. Once again, I naively set out to work. I transcribed dozens of interviews, formatted them into Q&A blog posts, took photos of the interviewees, and prepared them to be published. Despite my efforts, I later learned the by-line on these posts would not be my name. Instead they would be the name of the intern who conducted the interviews. As was with the daily reports I had written previously, I couldn't publicly claim my work. I had thought taking on this project would give me a level of credibility that would increase my opportunities; instead, it only showed I was willing to do grunt work without the credit.

When I requested the opportunity to publish a story under my name, I was rejected again. The deputy director doubled down on her reason: I didn't have a college degree. My lack of credentials reflected a lack of credibility and thus lack of capacity. My logical brain wanted to understand, but I couldn't help but feel as if I just wasn't good enough. I had proved my worth over and over again, but I still felt unworthy. I started to wonder if there was something else "wrong" with me. A closer look at the office internship program confirmed my suspicions.

The interns who worked in our office writing articles were usually graduate students from a writing program, though occasionally there would be undergraduates. I was a full-time employee and I was pursuing an associate degree. The interns were seen as capable because of their pursuit of a four-year or master's education, whereas my two-year degree was not seen as good enough. I rationalized this in my mind – it made sense in a way. But it was impossible to ignore the fact that, with the exception of a couple of Asian-American students (one of whom had a father working upstairs in our building in a high-level executive position), all the interns were white. No one questioned their ability to write a simple blog post.

My frustration grew, and the deputy director knew it. She frequently went out of her way to make sure I understood I was beneath her. I wasn't her assistant, yet she frequently asked me to complete tasks for her, such as mailing her letters. She made it clear she didn't like her direct reports taking breaks or eating lunch with me. I suspected the color of my skin or my age was to blame. I'd felt othered, and it was disheartening to know my hard work was overlooked. I was just "the paper girl."

Things came to a head when a new intern arrived. At our weekly department meeting, the deputy director introduced him with more fanfare than usual. He was the son of a colleague. I knew nepotism happened sometimes. But, interestingly to me, he was not a college graduate – not even a college student; he was in high school, and he was white. When I'd heard that, my face began to swell up; I was angry. All of the rejections I had faced finally came crashing down on me. My blood boiled to learn a

102

sixteen-year-old white boy was given more respect and more privilege, after I had more than proven my worth. I excused myself from the conference room, went to the bathroom, and cried. I thought I would never be good enough. My grandmother's words swirled around in my head: you have to work twice as hard to get half of what they are freely given. I cried harder when I remembered she also told me: working hard is still not a guarantee.

I left work that day with a new attitude. Though I was upset, I could finally see my reality. I realized I had started to believe I wasn't good enough. It was my lack of credentials; that was the thing that undermined all my credibility. I felt worthless and undervalued. I started withdrawing at work and wondering if others saw me in the same way as I had come to believe about myself. I second guessed all my actions and interactions with my coworkers. I didn't reach out for support because even thinking of a person in a superior position as potentially racist seemed to be a serious accusation. As Black women, we are taught in this world to constantly second guess ourselves, to ignore our gut reactions and to take abuse that stems from both racism and misogyny. Rocking the boat can be dangerous to our livelihoods, so, out of fear, we don't do it.

This fear can be so deep, we sometimes talk ourselves into wondering if there was even a problem at all to begin with, or worse, if we are the problem. After realizing this, I had called my grandmother and told her she had been right all this time. I wasn't good enough nor would I ever be for those who saw me as less than because of the color of my skin, my pedigree, or my lack of credentials. As always, she didn't sugar coat things. She asked me what I was going to do about it.

At first, my options didn't seem appealing. I'd worked at this university because it was safe. I was a single parent who needed the money and benefits. I didn't make moves because I didn't have a safety net to keep me afloat. I was renting an apartment in the Bay Area. With forty percent of my income going to rent and fifteen percent going to childcare, I was living paycheck to paycheck. It was overwhelming to think of what would happen if I lost this job.

Still, I pushed myself to reevaluate what exactly it was that I wanted to do in the world and do with my life. Did I want to be an administrative associate indefinitely? Could I settle into a lifelong career as the "the paper girl," one in which I would be looked down on daily? Was I comfortable being the only Black person in an entire office? Between my anxiety and tears, I learned the answers to these questions were no. I needed to do me, so I decided I couldn't work there anymore.

I want to be the person I was meant to be in this world. At a young age, I had learned quickly that I didn't want to be a person who allows myself to be held down by others, especially those who are afraid of my melanin, my brightness and my brilliance. Opportunities won't just present themselves – I needed to decide what opportunities I wanted and then seek them out. At this job, my world was small, and it wasn't a career I had wanted. My aspirations were beyond this position. I had been surviving my whole life. Now I wanted to thrive, not just survive.

At the time I came to these revelations, I was active in volunteering in criminal justice reform efforts in the Bay Area, especially those focused on the experiences of families impacted by incarceration. It was something I was and still am passionate about. I'd researched what a career as an attorney would offer me, and I decided it was something I wanted to move forward with.

Though I wasn't finished with the community college courses I needed to transfer to a four-year university, I committed to trying. I needed to make moves. The process of applying to universities and quitting my job filled me with anxiety. I had been immersed in an environment where I was told I was less than. Transferring that attitude into my new endeavors had been a real risk. Though, it wasn't as risky as continuing to stay in a position where I was treated with racism and discrimination, as well as having my skills questioned. I had been told for years that my lack of credentials meant I wasn't credible. So, getting those credentials now became my priority. And using those credentials to uplift others became my goal.

I wasn't treated poorly by everyone at that job. Numerous colleagues advocated for me, supported me and wanted me to succeed. I kept these people close – they became my tribe. When it came time to submit applications to universities, these same white coworkers edited my personal statements, helped me study, and even paid for my applications. I learned that though I faced obstacles in the workplace, there were those who genuinely cared about my success and did not care about the color of my skin. I learned to ask for help and push aside any shame or fear I had about accepting it. Ultimately, this help paid off. I was accepted into a great university with a substantial financial aid package that allowed me to quit my position and move into family housing with my young son. The day I'd found out I was accepted to the University of California in Santa Cruz was a pivotal moment of clarity.

I was at work sitting at my desk. I opened the email and felt a rush of happiness wash over me. *I was good enough!* I thought to myself. I let out a small shriek of joy – I couldn't believe it. My coworkers rushed to congratulate me. As they hugged me and offered their good wishes, the deputy director who blocked my opportunities got up from her desk and slammed her door. At that moment, I didn't care if she thought I was good enough to publish a story or good enough to take on more responsibility. I made decisions to make my life better and to seek the education and career I actually wanted. It didn't matter what other people thought of me; the only thing that mattered is what I thought of myself.

This moment was a few years ago and as I reflect on it now, as I'm about to graduate from the University of California, with the highest honors, I think about the writing opportunities passed over me in that job as I'm now writing a thesis about a complex topic I like. I'm also applying to law school. Not only will I have my BA, someday I will have my JD, and no one will tell me my credentials aren't good enough. If they say I'm not capable, I know it won't be because I don't have that little piece of paper that says I am. It will be because someone has a prejudice or preconceived notion of what I as a Black woman can do in this world.

My future holds plenty of people who will continue to question what I can and can't do. But I'll be prepared for it because I've learned no one can dictate what I am capable of or not. I have choices to make about what type of future I will have. I've learned to take risks to reach the things I want. As Black women, we are held to higher standards than others in the workplace. Our credibility will always be questioned, and a lack of credentials will make it easy for others to place the blame on us for not having them. Credentials give some level of credibility. Without them, we are told we are not good enough. With them, we may still be told we are not good enough, but at least this reveals the real reason behind being passed over for opportunities, promotions or more pay – racism.

To my fellow Black women who are facing racism at work, look at your situation and be honest with yourself about how you operate in your workplace. Are you following your passions? Are you happy or content? Is this where you want to be next year, the next five years, the next ten years? If you want to stay there and work it out, then do so knowing that your job does not define your worth as a human, let alone as a Black woman. You are worthy just by being you.

If you decide your job isn't working for you, then decide what will work for you. Do you need to go to school to get that credential you think you need that will help you get ahead in your field or another field you are passionate about? Make the leap – switch jobs, take risks, ask your network for support. You don't just have to utilize your professional network – ask your family and friends because the old school network of people you know will always support you. For Black women, there are scholarships and financial aid opportunities. Go and get that BS, MBA, Ph.D, or JD. Look for those financial opportunities to help you and have faith that they exist.

And finally, where there are people holding you down, there will be others trying to hold you up. Find those people, bring them into your circle and don't be afraid or ashamed to accept their support. You deserve it.

My grandmother has always told me to remember my worth and to be proud of my Blackness. So, I pass this on to you, too. Remember your worth, always. I don't care if you're a CEO or an administrative assistant – you are worthy of having the life you want to live. Positive self-talk and self-care are the most important. You are Black woman magic, perseverance and beauty. You are brains and wisdom. Do you, but always do it by loving yourself as you are.

Micro-aggression Veiled in a Hijab

April S. McLamb, RN, LCSW

HOW DOES AN act of modesty turn into an indecent event? How does an act of solidarity turn into an emotional and traumatic assault? I will tell you how. It all starts with a hijab. Some of you may not know the purpose of a hijab, but the hijab is a modest representation or way of showing society that the person wearing it is respecting themselves and asking society to indirectly respect them back. Unfortunately, the hijab is not always "welcomed" as an accepting form of attire. With that being said, I came across an event that occurred on February 1, 2018 that is called "World Hijab Day." I learned three valuable things the hard way: racial microaggressions are subtle in the workplace, how not to respond when faced with confrontation, and I can't talk about my concerns as a woman of color in the workplace without coming across as an "angry, Black woman."

In 2016, I moved to a rural community in Alaska. I was very particular on how I was going to wear my hair after this decision. Before I moved to Alaska, I decided to wear head wraps as an accessory to different outfits I would wear to work. I did some research on "tasteful" head wrap looks in the workplace and I was very excited about this venture because it was going to give me an opportunity to rebrand myself and show my self-expression of what my African identity means to me. African head wraps have always signified a symbol of regality to honor an African woman. So, during the first year of living in this rural village in Alaska, I'd worn a head-wrap almost every day.

One morning, I woke up to get ready for work and as I was perusing through social media, I learned that in different parts of the world people were celebrating hijabs. "World Hijab Day" is a day for people to show solidarity in dismantling the stigmatism of women of color wearing hijabs. So, since I had often worn headwraps, not hijabs, I thought I would show my solidarity by wearing one that day too. I called one of my coworkers who had worn hijabs for religious reasons and asked for her advice on wearing one. I did not want to be disrespectful toward her religious practices or those of anyone else. My coworker stated that she would wear her hijab as well, and thought it was a great idea.

When I had arrived at the office, to my surprise, upon opening the door to my office I found two of our supervisors sitting in my space. One supervisor, whom we will call Michelle for the sake of this writing, immediately blurted out, "Whoa, did I miss something? Is it Ramadan?" I suddenly was livid and saddened all at the same time. I found this statement offensive for two reasons: my supervisor knew very well where I stood in my religious beliefs, and she was aware of my head wrap use for the past two years. I remember once explaining to her, when I started working at the company, why I wore head wraps. Shocked at my supervisor's statement, I stood in place, frozen in disbelief that our supervisor was asking us this question. My emotions shifted and I now felt both attacked and humiliated. I also felt bad for my coworker who did celebrate Ramadan. I also knew that the celebration of Ramadan is much, much more than wearing a hijab. This entire scene was an example of racial microaggression taking place right before my very eyes.

I did not immediately respond to my supervisor when she posed the racist question to myself and my colleague. I simply replied, "No, it isn't Ramadan. Michelle, you know that I don't celebrate Ramadan." Michelle laughed it off and went on to explain to us why she was waiting in our office and moved the conversation forward. I can't quite exactly tell you what the rest of my day was like. Right now, it seems like it amounted to a big blur, but what I do remember was "stewing" in my anger and disbelief of how I had refrained from going off on Michelle.

I did not yell, argue, or curse her out because I did not want to portray the stereotypical angry, Black woman. Often, Black women are placed in a category of being bossy, mean, and angry. I did not want to send this message to my company or my colleagues. What I did do was something my mother had taught me when I'd first started working at the age of sixteen. I'd written the incident down in my notepad and kept a record of all the concerns I had experienced at this job in order to use this again if needed, when a situation arose where I was in front of upper management or human resources. One of the worst things I have felt as a woman of color is silencing my voice because it is often misunderstood. Sometimes this tactic is exhausting, often times I just want to yell and scream at the person and move on with my day, but as a Christian, African American woman, I hold myself to another set of standards that doesn't allow me to move and operate in chaotic ways, but handle myself in strategic ways that polishes and presents a sense of excellency in my professional life.

Modesty is closely related to humility. Humility is the state of freedom from pride or arrogance. In my racial microaggression encounter, I was met with arrogance and ignorance, but the mere fact I was wearing a hijab that promotes modesty and humility allowed me to turn my direction and passion toward something much greater, an act in kind to ensure that the representation of myself, my family, and my professional life remained intact in spite of what others might say or do in response to me. There are times when I become very overwhelmed and feel depleted due to the injustices I am faced with, but I stop and think about my legacy and what it will say about me when I am gone. This mere thought pushes me to continue to move forward as I wade through the microaggressions that will continue to be hurdled at me in this lifetime. It is my hope that my legacy will say, "She died empty because she gave it her all."

Don't Burn Bridges

Terryann Nash, MA

THERE WAS A time when Black people weren't allowed to "cross bridges" for the sake of protest. The reason being, it would have cost them their lives even though protesting injustice is a fundamental right. In honor of my ancestors, I have made it my mission to try and dismantle white supremacy systems. If I am burning a bridge, then may I burn 1,000 bridges times 1,000 and in turn, create bridges that will bring about change!

I want to start by saying the racial disparities are shameful in Minnesota. The top three distinctions that I contend with are:

1. We have one of the most extended probationary oversight/reporting systems in the country. People here are on probation up to ten times longer even more than Conservative states

2. Only 20% of the population of color have four-year degrees or any type of higher education

3. 20% of the BIPOC own property

These facts prove that Blacks (and people of color) were never seriously considered when it came to community investment and financial equity. It is my belief as a second-generation Minnesotan that BIPOC became a select type of chattel. This protected class appeared on paper for the mere sake of gaining financial security for whites, that continues to uphold a Jim Crow system that guarantees a bright future for their children at the expense of the brown ones around them.

In Minnesota, the civil rights era was a new era with the same old unspoken rules and expectations. The schools were desegregated in 1971, and the first Black mayor was elected in 1994. If you played the game and knew your *place and* stayed within it, fluidity amongst the approved ranks appeared to work in your benefit. A scenario where if you've ever heard the saying "The Devil is in the details," would be a case in which making a distinction between the two would be merely impossible.

As a native, I'd discovered the disparities as I've lived them. I became aware of the educational system's gaps as I would often be separated from my friends to find myself one of few in larger white settings — the beginning of my "acceptable" behavior training. When I'd started working in the workplace, I'd seen the hidden rules of promotion and upward mobility to those who were in the position that worked toward pleasing the boss, even when covering for their inadequacies and qualifications. Lastly, was the unspoken conduct to surviving in a covert racially hostile environment; keep smiling, share little and never fraternize. All cogs in the system of white supremacy dressed up in social and human resource policies that transcends corporate America. In most cases, human resources will attempt to make you feel heard, but they are there to make sure they fire you within the company's legal rights. For the record, I've once had an excellent HR manager who did work on behalf of all the employees. Unfortunately, she was undermined by her boss. I like to call HR the "elephant in the room." They tend to uphold the status quo, which makes them part of the problem.

Minnesota's vast dichotomy between its Blacks and whites sometimes makes it challenging to distinguish tokenism in the workplace right away. It is not uncommon to have workplace settings where 98% of the staff are white or where there may be a fair number of diverse line staff with all management being white. I have often had the best interviews, saying all the right things, and landing the job. This is problematic due to tokenism and the expectation that you will fall into ranks and "know" your place. This covert climate is tolerated because that same job is more than a check, a house, a car, it's your status in the community.

My workplace story started when I'd decided I wanted to pursue a new career because I needed to make more money. I applied to numerous places, and as I look back, I see my first mistake was not elevating my sights. I had been in school for a few years and had not realized I had never changed my job description to reflect my current skill set. I applied to several jobs and went on interviews that went fairly well. In the end, I had three job offers, all with similar pay ranges, benefits, and location. I decided to select an agency that I had a long-standing relationship with. I chose this agency for two main reasons: The location and the fact that I would have a Black woman as a supervisor. I was so excited because I knew I could do the job, and I thought it would be cool to work "hands-on" again with the community.

My first week on the job was pretty awesome. I was introduced to staff, employees, and given the royal treatment. The job even came with covered parking. Looking back, I see it as "the bait to the switch," or the honeymoon stage.

The second week, the company decided to do some downsizing and announced we would be moving. After turning down my first choice, that was an equal distance from my house, but a bit less money. I would now commute twenty-seven minutes each way instead of seven. There would be no office with a desk, but instead a cubicle in the back of the room. No lovely professional building, but a community center rejected site. It was obvious, I had made the wrong choice, but I decided I would make the best of this situation. I gave myself the timeline of a year to graduate and find another job.

So now, here I am in my new location and immersed in "culture." We had the look of an agency of color, but the powers that had made a gradual shift, and all the weight was at the bottom. Two were in command and both were white, while neither qualified. Whites controlled the boundaries... starting with keeping their offices separate from ours. The management team would come out of their ivory tower office space to venture down to the plantation and rub elbows with the brown employees here and there. The office environment was set up so that if the area were ever compromised, the active shooter would be out of bullets before he would get to any BIPOC's.

The seating arrangement *was* the culture (wink). They called it "family culture" but it felt more like ownership. I also saw that ownership was not "acceptance." They created a relationship that appeared to be one of approval. This "acceptance" was really an invisible fence of ownership, subtly dictating what was to be acceptable behavior and culture for the relationship to become or remain relevant. Everything was being run and controlled in a small, tight, yet very superficial manner.

It was okay for me to work on a project that would solve a problem and improve my job output: I would tackle the problem and get it done, and the clients were happy. Yet upon review, my supervisor: Katrina, would insinuate that I was struggling with prioritizing my work when, in fact, I had exceeded the expectations.

I found that every day was a different case. I had not only picked the wrong job, but I'd also chosen the wrong supervisor. There was a second woman of color who had managed another department of four staff members. She was kind and cared about her team. The way she'd run her department was pretty slick, she understood the environment, and she was genuine about her staff's growth and development.

I, on the other hand, had selected the queen of the gas-lighters–Katrina. She was the supervisor of a one-person department

— me. Her job was to train and encourage others, but behind the scenes she did and said things about the people she'd worked with that was contrary to the company's "best practices" (no gossiping). This chick knew her stuff well; she didn't have to study for she was a natural. I would go so far as to call her a master instructor in the field.

Her narcissism made her a pro at what she'd done. In another place in time, I would bet money that she was an "overseer" in the traditional sense. The overseers, we're unable to settle conflict within the ranks, but somehow see their acceptance as a badge of honor that they wildly brazened around the plantation. The overseer's main responsibility is to carry out the corporate owners' orders while keeping the status quo of the "balanced plantation," and she executed that very well.

Katrina often participated in "code-switching." She would usually address me as Ms., but when talking about her supervisor, she gave the appearance that she was in control and would talk a bit more candidly. I was to be her trusty assistant and we were going to become a dynamic duo. I was called a "Linchpin" and I was excited to prove she was right. I knew that I was overqualified and believed it was possible to make this a successful endeavor. Katrina was very self-confident and gave me the impression that she was in control of her department expansions. I later discovered — she was not. I became too comfortable. I was excited to work with a woman of color and more excited to have her as my supervisor. I thought this would be a genuine opportunity. I thought I'd found a haven of sorts, and I intended to strive to be a "right-hand" of an assistant. Be careful what you ask for...

Katrina was like a hurricane starving for power all strung out on herself. She was above company rules and did not always follow them; if she "liked" you, she would impose upon policies then considered it off the record. For instance, I was taken to lunch (with drinks), encouraged to leave early (when I said I had work to do), and taken to a clearance shoe sale all during work hours to later be told that I was not prioritizing my time.

I would routinely advocate for clients' assistance to then be denied. Later others who did not always earn it would be granted special variances for a story most likely to sell more tickets at the annual event or be the best poster story to get favor over mine. Her way pleased the powers above her as she executed her petty deeds to keep the "negros" in check. The acceptance she'd sought made me sick. I saw Katrina perpetuating the same plantation mentality of the slave master.

My final straw was the constant inquiries regarding my hair. Being that I have locks that fall to the middle of my back, I decided I would *never* wear my hair uncovered due to the environment. This particular supervisor was always asking me about my hair and complimenting me on how pretty it was. I'd often told her I didn't feel comfortable wearing my hair down and that it was more professional in the workplace to keep it up. After seeing this woman touch the hair of another woman, I kept my hair tied up and contained.

Katrina's supervisor was transparent in her role, and it would not be uncommon for the "white" woman to run her hands through Katrina's weekly parade of wigs (without even asking). This behavior terrified me, as I knew one day it may happen to me, and I would be done. So, I always covered my hair and reiterated that I didn't like people to touch it whenever I could, to avoid such interactions. It was an incident of this nature that ultimately led to my departure from the company.

My perspective for sharing this workplace story is that we are often thrust into environments perceived or observed as unhealthy, creating, or continuing to perpetuate all stereotypes that ostracize us (people of color) from such settings. If we are quiet and allow our spaces to be imposed upon, then it will be at the expense of our dignity. We aren't pets. Once that line is crossed, it sets a tone of what is now acceptable. I just knew that gaslighting Katrina was going to set her straight in one of those tones she'd often practiced on me, instead I was left bewildered by what I'd experienced. It was definitely second hand trauma, a real trigger. Where I come from, (white) people touching on you without invitation is a violation. My heart sank and I had a lump in my throat as I hurried to excuse myself.

I now had approximately two months on the job, and we had moved to a new location. I thought everything was going well. I thought this was my time to step up and show my worth. Realizing that my supervisor lived further away than I did, I would get to work early and try to set up our classroom, greet any clients that came in first, and get my work done. Often my supervisor would rush in late. She would appear to be a bit chaotic and would even be a little short with me. Although she would say "thank you," it never felt genuine. Most of the time, the "thank you" was given after cutting me off or dismissing me from the group.

I attempted to study her to try and figure out her nuances and genuinely become an asset to the process. It felt like the more I had done, the more I needed to do, and she was never really satisfied. She often gave me a directive, and when I had attempted to do it, I would find that she had already done it. These actions would occur even with simple tasks such as emails. I would often double-check before doing things because I wanted to make sure that my learning process was accurate in an effort to not make any future errors. My supervisor informed me that my continued quest for information was annoying and that I should put everything in writing and just read the emails. Some of the systems were new, and merely reading an email did not always suffice when going through a systematic process. So, I had set out to be my best client and prepare my own training plan, which included other employees who had been employed there for years and had worked directly with my program.

119

It was in this process that I'd found that not only was I doing the job but that the supervisor had added extra tasks to my job that no one else knew of or was doing, which would appear to be extra work. Once I had realized this, I decided to come in early to get ahead of the game, learn the job, and not have to rely on the supervisor for little details.

This was a problem as well, and I was then questioned about my hours (being too long), although I was salaried and told that my time stops when my work is done. It got to the point that it felt every time I turned around Katrina was nitpicking or had a discrepancy.

When I would step in the classroom to observe her, she felt that my job was to wait in the hallway for the clients once they were excused, if I had stepped into the classroom to offer any comment or ask a question I was often ignored right in front of clients. My conclusion that things weren't going in my favor was when I had requested to go to a conference in between sessions. I believed that this conference was part of the training topics being presented at the workplace (EI). Still, because I had a conversation (in passing with her supervisor) regarding the keynote speaker lineup, it was perceived that I had bucked her authority. Therefore, I would not be allowed to use any work time for the training.

After attempting to explain to her several times that I did not buck her authority and I was merely discussing the topic with the supervisor in our afternoon conversation and that *she* became excited about it and thought it was an excellent idea that I attend. My supervisor was so upset that I talked to her supervisor when she was gone (even though everyone was talking to her, during her pageant stroll from the ivory tower). When I had brought it to her, I'd learned she did not want me talking to anyone at all. I'd expected not to interact with other staff, but to just come in and do my job only to speak to my supervisor and go home. This treatment lasted for about ninety days until I'd decided I would confide in a so-called friend at school...

During the holiday season, I was feeling pretty bad. I had a lot of things on my plate, and I was a bit overwhelmed. My job was having a holiday party, but I needed to be somewhere else for a family emergency, so I left early. During that holiday weekend, I saw a so-called friend at school who happened to pass herself off as a professional. I had reached out to her for professional advice regarding my family member, and I had shared the frustrations that I was going through on my job with her. I'd just witnessed something that I thought was terrifying, and I just wanted to vent. I asked my friend for advice because I felt that if there was anything I could do differently on my job to yield better results, I was willing to try it. I happened to mention that my boss and her supervisor seem to have boundary issues that I felt were unacceptable. I'd mentioned to her how my boss often talked about her supervisor yet acted differently when she came around. I even went as far as to say that seeing my boss operate in this manner not only made me uncomfortable around her, but I was very disappointed in her and was not sure if I could respect her as I had before. I sincerely wanted to try and improve our professional dynamics.

I may have gone a bit far in my supervisor's judgment, but I honestly thought I was talking to someone I could trust, and it felt so good to get it all off my chest. When we finished, I thanked her, and we hugged. Sometimes it's best to suck it up and keep your mouth shut that's what I'd learned! My job went from bad to worse all over a holiday weekend at school. Things got ugly at my job.

I'd left that weekend, receiving a text from my supervisor stating that I was awesome and thanking me for all the work I had done, that made me feel really good. I thought I had turned a page, and I was ready to run. Oddly, three days later, I had received another text stating that my work was inadequate and that I would need to come in and have a meeting with HR. I had arrived at work (on Monday) to find all of my files had been pulled, and each of my duties was being scrutinized item by item — picking each one of them apart. Katrina wanted to paint a picture that I could not do my job and that my work was behind. However, when I got her email, texts, and voicemail, I knew that something was up, so I decided to report to work early and get all my stuff together. When I got to the meeting, I'd brought all my paperwork with me to show that much of my job had been done and that I was actually right on track.

Katrina then stated we had a "communication problem" and that she would like to see us working better together and that I was not to talk to any other staff members regarding how to do my job or what my job duties were. She then told me my job depended on my ability to get along with my supervisor. Huh?

I'd pointed out that I was unaware of any miscommunications due to prior texts and emails, in which I was informed I was doing a good job. HR questioned Katrina, who then asked if we could then extend a thirty-day professional improvement plan toward working on better communication and best work practices. Everything I had done became a matter of scrutiny. Katrina continued to go behind my back questioning anything I had said to staff members, and once I walked into the cubicle area and sat at my desk while I listened to her talk to other staff members about me. I confronted her in a meeting. She denied it.

Katrina became my workplace bully, she began interfacing with my assigned clients on an individual basis, circumventing my work with the clients. She made attempts to downplay my job and was often annoyed when clients would come in for intake, and I would know many of them from my twenty-five years of community development and organization experience. She did not like me!

At the end of this particular day, I learned that she had been privy to the conversation I had and the so-called friends at school. She began to make references to my conversation in front of a large group of people. I'd attempted to speak to her directly, but she chose not to address me in that manner. I told her if there's anything you've ever heard that you have a question of, please feel free to ask me. But this only became fuel to her fire!

Katrina took pride in doing the overseer's work. Her supervisor also began to avoid me and the supervisor's supervisor, John, became rude in his manner of trying to ignore me while interacting with other staff members. It was apparent that not only was she pissed about my conversation, but she was twisting anything I may have said or asked her in the past to create a hostile environment.

Her goal was to turn the environment against me. This Black woman made a conscious effort to disparage another Black woman to white people without discussion. How sad. What made this even more tragic was my words had been taken out of context by someone I didn't realize had an issue with me. The whole thing was juvenile in nature and crazy in reality.

One day John brought in a colleague, which happened to be a good friend of mine. While sitting in my cubicle, I observed him introducing her to everyone around but skipped me. I patiently waited until they were all done, and while retrieving a document from the copy center, we caught a glance. She immediately shouted my name and ran toward me, giving me the biggest friendliest hug ever. John later questioned me as to how did I know her?

I wasn't sure how much longer I would be able to take such abuse. Not only was I feeling it, but it was very obvious to my coworkers who continue to question it. I thought it was just sad that we could come into a work environment that we know is controlled by people who don't look like us and don't have our best interest at heart, but yet we fall in and play their games and give them the power to abuse us.

I held out as long as I could. I had a few things working in my favor, but I knew I was quitting this job. The first thing was I had a foot surgery scheduled that would take me out for a few weeks, which then put me closer to my graduation date, which put me closer to summer, and I'd be out of there by April—that was my goal.

I went out for foot surgery. The healing process was prolonged an extra two weeks. When I returned from foot surgery, I was not allowed to see any clients or meet any new clients. I was told not to schedule any meetings, and all of my financial resources were redistributed to other employees; some not even working with clients directly. My last day, my keys were confiscated, I was locked out of my files, and left to sit at my desk looking at the wall. After three hours of this treatment, Katrina called a meeting with me and the new HR representative. I knew what time it was, and I was okay with it. Katrina sat with a big smile spread across her face. She pulled out a piece of paper and read a litany of lies. She then told me nothing was up for discussion and that due to my "over recruiting," I was fired! That was the best day ever for me on that job.

Although I've never been to Africa or on any exotic safaris, I feel that I've explored "the elephant in the room" like situations in my mind. It is not uncommon. The outcomes are very different based on individual circumstances and perceptions recorded in management grievances. In other words, what white coworkers do and what Black coworkers do and get away with, it will never be the same. That's one of the rules of corporate America's unspoken Jim Crow "Separate but equal" policies.

My corporate American experience is the backdrop to how we, as people of color, are used against each other in the workplace. Solidarity is out due to the mistrust we cannot solve even our most simple problems (he said, she said) without finding the need for approval from the big house. When these disparities in our personal lives overflow into our workplaces, it gives insight as to why I now live in a town that will be historically known as the "epicenter" of racial disparities and deadly police force. Minnesota is now an epicenter to the world on the real impact of corporate discrimination. It can never be said enough. Corporate discrimination is more than a dream put on layaway, but the fatal submission of existence. A continual knee to our neck!

I saw my exit like a golden parachute. I am on my own. I no longer answer to what I know is *not* my calling. I have stepped out on faith and the view has been incredible. I have grown in this experience to have faith in my God and trust in myself. I have met incredible people, and I can honestly say that I don't have the answers and may not have my HR department, but I am truly happy, even in the unknown. I am confident that my success is my professional destiny that is aligned for me to step into. I am not defined by systems that don't love me or recognize my worth. I am living a Nash inspired life.

PS: Twelve hours after my termination for "over recruiting" the office was closed due to Covid-19.

The Delusion Effect of Racism

Nora Wood

WHEN I RECEIVED the news that I had obtained my dream job as a Program Coordinator responsible for creating a brand-new program at a non-profit community clinic in a growing urban city, I was absolutely elated. This job would allow me to use my knowledge and experience to design a program in the short span of a three-month deadline and I was anxious to get started. I had grown up knowing that I had to work twice as hard as my white counterparts to achieve the same goals that seemed to be handed to them as part of their privilege. This was instilled in me throughout my childhood. However, I was determined to remain optimistic throughout this process. I was ready to conquer the world and climb the tall mountain to make an impact as a successful Black woman from a small rural town. Little did I know that as a Black woman, my dream to serve would be impacted not by my education and credentials but simply by the color of my skin. It was a rude awakening for me because this would be the first time my career would be impacted by racism. Honestly, I truly didn't realize how racism existed in the workplace in this millennium before then.

I grew up in a small Southern town and attended a Christian private elementary school where I was one of only three Black children. I got along well with my white classmates and they remain my friends still to this day. I really never experienced racism in my younger years. To coin an old phrase – "we all just got along." No, I never really thought about or experienced racism in my little corner of the world. I know that may seem strange, especially since I live in the South in the state that was the first to secede from the Union in 1860 and where the first shot of the Civil War was fired. Maybe because we are a small town with an important history of our participation in the American Revolutionary War, we insulated ourselves from the rampant typical Southern racism that surrounded us. Don't misunderstand me, racism exists in our small town in pockets where certain types of demographics display it openly and proudly, but it is not widespread or common.

I had arrived wide-eyed and ready to work in this big and fast-growing city. I envisioned changing this facility to meet the challenges this new program would bring, but I did not realize that my vision would be drastically changed. When I walked in the door on my first day, I was greeted by the office manager who stated that "You are one of us cousin, so I have to look out for you." I had the feeling that this was my first clue to what was awaiting me as I began this new adventure. The second Black woman at the office also greeted me stating she was happy to have me as a part of the staff. It was when I was greeted by the white women in the office, I'd noticed a distinct difference in their welcoming. There was a distinctive hesitation in even extending the greeting and I was not greeted as a welcomed new employee but simply as a replacement for the person who had held the job prior to me. They even added in their comments "I hope you will be better than her." The old childhood feeling of here we go again, having to prove I will be better and more worthy of this achievement not because I am qualified but simply because I am not white, began to creep in.

I was informed by the Black staff members that working here was the equivalent of navigating a race war on a daily basis and the division was so broad that Blacks were literally on one side of the table and whites were on the other side and it was especially prevalent during meetings and lunch. Had I walked into a time warp where the people from a backwoods racist rural area had invaded a metropolitan city and encapsulated it with racism? I also quickly realized that the majority of the clinicians were white women who were not licensed, nor did they possess credentials as advanced as mine. Yet these white women were in key managerial positions and in charge of managing the staff and caseloads. The Black women on staff were mainly in clerical positions even though some had degrees in social work.

I have always been the person who would make the best of any situation that I happen to be a part of at any given time. I would seek out the strengths of a situation and continue to work as I normally would. I had approached this job with the attitude that I would make the best of an indelicate situation because I was here to launch my new program designed to assist clients who really needed the help, clients who were mainly Black and needed someone who could relate to their experiences. It was also what I had worked so hard to achieve in earning my education and licensing credentials. This was the goal I had dreamed of accomplishing so no matter what I would prevail.

As I worked my caseload and built my clientele, I was approached by the clinical manager with a proposition that would add additional tasks to my workload. It would start with drafting a job description for the position I was currently working in as it was newly created specifically for me due to my credentials. The other task was for me to learn the electronic monitoring system as a lead clinician. He then stated that since I was the only licensed clinician on staff that I would be tasked with finding additional sources of funding for the program. My first thought was how much work can be placed on one person to accomplish? I'd wondered why this was being done specifically to me. I asked myself the question of whether my race was once again playing a part in his process of how he made this decision to assign me these particular tasks.

After working in my new lead clinical position for a few days, I made an appointment to meet with the clinical supervisor to discuss my additional roles, the responsibility for an intern and the training required for the electronic monitoring system with its processes. My supervisor was a fifty-year old white woman who employed a biting and edgy form of sarcasm when you were having a discussion with her. I was hesitant to discuss anything with her but felt like I needed to give her a chance in spite of our previous encounters that were laced with strong negativity and the undercurrent of racism. I needed the system training and was willing to endure her edgy behavior in order to accomplish that goal. When talking with her over the phone she seemed excited to help, in addition to knowing that the facility would be receiving financial reimbursements for the cases I'd handled as the sole licensed clinician. I would be a source of income for the clinic. However, getting my supervisor to actually meet became more of an effort than working my actual job. I soon realized I was getting the run around while starting to feel I was being set up to fail.

I quickly decided to ask the other clinicians who had years of experience to train me on the monitoring system process. That quickly revealed their ability to stall the process and give me the run around with constant excuses or time constraints.

When I was finally able to hold a meeting with this supervisor about my training, I was told that I had enough letters behind my name with a fancy license and should be able to figure out how to work the system on my own. That statement stunned me because it showed a side to my supervisor that indicated her true frame of mind about me. I indicated to her that my having a license should not have any bearing on learning the workings of the system employed in the clinic. As usual her disgust was evident on her face as she rolled her eyes in reaction to what I stated. I am a professional and my personality insists on knowing the rules and processes of the job I have been given. I had to maintain a high level of composure and professionalism throughout the meeting even though I was on the verge of tears. Once again, the feelings of being set up for failure returned and in trying to understand what was going on, I was also feeling crushed by the indignity of enduring what was now full-blown racism. I had to remind myself that since I was a licensed and credentialed clinician, they needed me especially since I could bring in revenue through reimbursement for my services. I concentrated on how I could find some way to learn the process since it was becoming increasingly clear no one was going to train me.

I returned to my office after this meeting and closed the door. I took some deep breaths and thought through what had just occurred. I was being asked to complete various tasks and procedures when there would be no training on the process to accomplish the assignment. There was never any intention to train me properly. She just wanted to provide me with a caseload to work and walk away. I felt as though I may have been overreacting to the situation so I needed to run the events by some colleagues I knew I could trust to give me their honest assessment. My colleagues validated my feelings about her behavior while indicating it was unacceptable and unnecessary. They also corroborated that she was being racist but acknowledged that at least she was open with it and did not attempt to hide it from plain view.

I had to learn to accept at face value that even though this agency was located in a fast growing, metropolitan city, they were not progressive, and diversity was not a real priority. It was quite a compromise for me, and I'd realized that change does not always happen just because you want it to occur. Only the white women who were there had been in the agency longer than anyone else and probably felt that training someone who was more credentialed than them would be intimidating. The only thing they could hold over me was their knowledge of the system and their processes. The entire time I had worked there, they would only dispense limited information while forcing me to continually ask questions about the procedures and policies. It was all about power and control that they felt due to their privilege they could use to their advantage. It once again reinforced that many white people do not think their actions of racism personally have any effect on others and they have every right to openly express their racist views and actions at any given time.

Throughout my experience, I've resolved to stay positive, but the incident did rattle and shake me to my core. The comments, the non-verbal cues, the facial grimaces with pure disgust weighed heavy on my spirit. At first, I'd felt I might be overreacting and that what had occurred could not be an act of racism. Maybe it was all just a misunderstanding or an honest disconnect due to the situation. I personally feel that acts of racism have a delusional effect that cause you to second guess if the individuals' actions are intentional or just done out of plain ignorance. During my experience, I had consulted with my colleagues to ensure I wasn't being delusional or overreacting. It has been my experience that individuals who express open racist traits like to place the blame on the victims which creates a traumatic incident. Victims of consistent racism often suffer from post-traumatic stress disorder in addition to other mental health issues.

Writing this essay on my experience has helped me find my voice and has given me the ability to speak out. I am hoping to help other young Black men and women entering into the workforce find a source of strength to overcome the struggle in combating racism. Corporate America and even just being an essential worker in other employment situations will not be kind or easily accepting of our abilities due to our skin color. I am feeling liberated at being able to express my feelings openly. I also stood up for myself against the racist individuals at my job site and outed their racist behavior both in this essay and in person.

Through this experience I have learned my *purpose*! I was there to help individuals who felt the same and shared similar experiences as mine. I have helped them to find their voice and inspired them to advocate for themselves against racist activity. I have not always had this passion to be the person who speaks out or advocates for herself, but I have learned over the course of time that I must be an advocate for myself while inspiring others to do the same. Racism always needs to be exposed, brought to the surface and self-advocacy brings it into the light of day while taking away the cover of darkness. Let's vow to expose racism at its core and create real change even if we do it one person at a time.

Get the Language Right

Danne Smith Mathis

> *"I want to get the language right tonight!"*
> **~The Late Dr. Martin Luther King, Jr.**

DURING HER ACCEPTANCE speech for the vice-presidential nomination at the Democratic National Conventions, Senator Kamala Harris said: *"The litmus test for America is how we treat Black women."* This is every person's test. It was a test my parents aced! I did not grow up in an abusive home. I'd never known or saw it and it was never a topic of discussion outside of our home. Ironically, however, after twenty-six years of faithful commitment inside of a marriage that was laced with abuse, I agreed to a divorce and re-entered the full-time workforce in 2010 as a proposal writer for an aerospace defense corporation. There, I was being trained by a nurturing boss, a white woman, Lisa Gunnison, who not only taught me the processes of proposal management and business development, but also more importantly, how to regain confidence in myself as a woman, a mother, and a professional. Fourteen months later, I was laid off after a corporate reorganization and lived on unemployment until one of the potential employers that initially rejected my resume, came back eight months later and offered me a full-time position as a proposal manager. This opportunity afforded me the chance to improve as not only a proposal management professional but also gave me lifelong friends. Moreover, the guidance I had received from a few of the coworkers who genuinely cared about me was priceless. After a year of employment, I received the company's highest award bestowed on exemplary employees annually, who align with the company's values and who have been instrumental in turning around some aspect of the company's operations. In my case, it was significantly reducing the turnaround time for the production of proposal responses. Afterward, I'd overheard conversations by fellow Black coworkers who did not know me at the time and who spoke of how easy it was to win the award; a statement that could not have been further from the truth. But the post-award conversation I remembered most was the one initiated by a fellow Black coworker who told me emphatically that because I had won the award, my corporate life was about to become hell and that I would eventually either resign or be fired!

My parents taught me the necessity of accepting people for who they are, so I'd embraced their mantra: "The difference in others makes no difference." They ingrained in me that weaknesses could be the foundation of gaining inner strength if I had learned how to recover quickly from inevitable mistakes with the least amount of harm to myself and others who may have been involved in the errors of my life. That was my reality. They ensured I knew how to discern my friends, my enemies, trusted advisors, and those who would fall somewhere in between. And while this curriculum of life prepared me for most everything that had been positive and successful during my early professional career, it did not prepare me for the myopic racism that flowed through the veins of corporate America years later. This life syllabus did not prepare me for the narrative that awaited me when I arrived as an evolved, strong, determined, and outspoken Black woman.

I began my first full-time job in 1975. I spent four college summers of gainful employment that was safeguarded by virtue of the fact that my employer was the institution where my father served as college president. During this time, I learned the treachery of politics and the treasure of trusted allies. I inhaled the knowledge of how politicians, legislators, and legislation worked in tandem to either advance or destroy a community. I entered corporate America after graduate school in 1982. It wasn't a typical position for a young person then. My immediate supervisor was the president and CEO of a major healthcare company in my New Jersey hometown and my father was a governor-appointee to the company's Board of Trustees. For me, it was like home- a place where I was safe and protected- a place where mistakes were readily forgiven, and discussions occurred about the lessons I learned from them. In 1987, I'd turned down an offer for a promotion, chose to start a family, and went out on maternity leave when I became pregnant with my first child. Then, I resigned in 1988 after serving as a proposal writing consultant during my postpartum stage after my decision to remain a stay-at-home mother. I'd homeschooled my three children for the next fifteen years. During that time, I had learned the art of developing long-lasting personal and professional relationships. My first lesson began at home- my place of protection, love, warmth, growth, and knowledge transfer. As a young adult, it was also the place where I'd learned to develop political, religious, and social views during discussions at the dinner table with my parents and two younger sisters. It was the place where I could verbalize my thoughts without censorship and judgment. It was the safe haven where I did not have to apologize for being Catholic, and Republican – two uncommon traits for a young Black person. It was the place where I'd embraced the diversity in our family -Caucasian in-laws, Italian godfathers, bi-racial relatives, and friends who were products of divorced parents- friends who learned how to swim at my home as my parents taught them how to navigate the waters of life.

I was unaware of our multi-ethnic family and never thought of myself as a person who'd grown up "Black." I was not a "Black" person. I was simply a person who grew within a family that gave me security, protection, and acceptance from people of all different ethnicities, levels of education, and socio-economic positions. From this, I'd also learned the value of mentorship as I've listened to my father coach his college administrators and faculty at our dinner table on many occasions. Ironically, most of my mentors were white women who helped me mature through various phases of my life. I had come to enjoy and expect this type and level of interaction with them and with that inevitably came a level of trust to which I had also become accustomed. It was a level of trust I had bestowed on women like the late Dr. Shirley Thomas, the daughter of an electrical engineer, a homemaker and a radio-television actress, writer, producer, author, and my professor in the Master of Professional Writing Program at the University of Southern California. The woman who forced me out of my comfort zone as a creative writer and taught me the necessity of technical writing. I'd learned to trust women like Patricia Branca, my college history professor who had written the book <u>Silent Sisterhood,</u> a study of Victorian women of the late 19th century in the home and in the family, the woman who nurtured me like a daughter after I'd left for college. I learned to trust women like Nancy Forbord, president of the Washington Association of Television and Children (W.A.T.C.H.), the woman who hired me as her writing assistant to edit the testimony she'd delivered to the Federal Trade Commission (FTC) as she advocated for increased children's television programming in the nation's capital before she picked up her children from school and went home to cook dinner for her family. These women, in tandem with my mother, helped me to develop my stance on the pursuit of motherhood and a career. Because of them I'd learned when, how and mainly why to fight for the good of my family without an apology!

Shortly after the merger and acquisition in 2015, my company re-organized and eliminated the position of the person that not only hired me in 2012, but who had also served as my corporate champion. When you have no champion in corporate America, you are weeded out and that is when I began to experience situations that were designed to change the narrative of me as "Momma D," the term of endearment given to me by my coworkers of all colors. It was re-written by two new white women supervisors who not only appeared to be threatened by me as a woman of color but also as a person who had built unique professional and personal relationships within the company. During this transition, I went from a respected award-winning employee to a performance improvement plan (PIP). Previously documented successes like managing the proposal project that translated into the company's largest win in its history and writing a proposal response that a procurement officer had called "The best and most well-written one he had read in all his career," became part of my erased history. The new supervisory duo engaged in activity that attempted to do what corporate America does to most Black women: paint them as angry and volatile employees in an effort to erase the threat they feel because of our intelligence and because of the emotional resilience we deploy against designed and intense daily scrutiny of our work. Their activity was also part of what appeared to be a deliberate attempt to marginalize not only my efforts to become part of the new team, but also my continued efforts to become a better employee. These attempts manifested themselves in such things as false accusations of me not getting along with others on RFP projects, accusations I was able to disprove personally through follow-up calls to the very employees they tried to turn against me. In addition, I was excluded from major conferences where critical information was communicated to our unit, conferences that previously had been mandatory for me to attend. And for the first time in my professional career, I was also met with an accusation of "not being forthright" during a situation where subject matter experts (SMEs) and sales staff who had known me as the company's only proposal manager, and who had not been briefed on the new organizational structure and new processes of our unit, forwarded me emails on an incoming RFP and not my two new supervisors. Thus, I was accused of deliberately hiding communications from my new boss, which suggested I deliberately proposed to keep her out of the loop even when I had forwarded her all the emails prior to her request for the same. The accusation was totally incongruent with my character. When I'd expressed my concerns over unfair criticism of my work and my efforts, I was accused of being "defensive." The language of this new and untrue narrative was frustrating and disheartening. Yet, I was determined to get it right not simply to prove a point but mainly to improve processes.

In order to improve anything, whether it be a conversation or a relationship- personal or professional- truth must be at the foundation of everything that drives it for the ultimate well-being of the entity; and the truth of the matter is that there is a legitimate time to be "defensive." Individuals make a living coaching such strategies. This is not understood in corporate America. To deploy a defensive strategy or response at any given time means there is a perceived need to protect against acts of aggression. This aggression is often passively applied in corporate America and antithetical to the culture of Black women who have had to fight clearly defined and exposed enemies for centuries. Nonetheless, I had proposed to make necessary and immediate adjustments. I discussed them during weekly check-in calls with my new supervisors and team members to whom I was ready and willing to transfer the knowledge I had gained during my seven years with the company, despite the fact that they were located together in another office in another state. This too, would become part of the new narrative of me as one of the new supervisors labeled me as the "remote employee" during a team call when in fact, I worked at the corporate headquarters office daily. I was painted as the outsider and felt like the unwanted stepchild. That had never been my reality neither inside nor outside of an office! Yet, I had learned to thrive in the loneliness of being the only member of my team on site by assuming roles apart from my hired position. I became co-chair of the Council on Diversity and Inclusion and leader of the Military Veterans and Friends Employee Resources Group. These positions represented other issues in life that were dear to my heart: equality and support of the military and military families.

In November 2017, nine months after my bilateral knee replacement and four months after I had just returned from family medical leave, I decided to help my daughter, a single mother, advance in her military career as an enlisted soldier in the United States Army during the last eight months of her duty tour in Okinawa, Japan. I flew there overnight to bring my fourteen-month old grandson (and only grandchild) home with me. While the decision did not seem a daunting task at the time, it would prove to be life changing. It would set the stage for my ultimate departure from this company. During that time, I rarely slept through the night and consequently and admittedly, my work suffered from a quality standpoint. Yet I was never given the benefit of the doubt even though this was clearly an aberration for me–a conscientious, professionally qualified, and dedicated employee–amidst an unusually extenuating circumstance. Thus, it became increasingly apparent that although I had worked with my supervisor and HR to put a work-from home accommodation in place the first two weeks of my grandson's transition, the execution of this agreement was met with what appeared to be resentment and disdain. It also appeared to me that support was clearly less than genuine and came from something other than a place of compassion and understanding. The values of diversity, respect, and compassion are oftentimes not endogenous to a company. This was evident with the continued emotional harassment that took the form of criticism about every little thing I did not accomplish to my supervisors' liking. It was an all too familiar scenario where I'd found myself questioning my own sanity like I did in my abusive marriage. Like then, I had once again found myself searching the internet to understand what I was experiencing. That is when I became aware of the term "gaslighting." This situation reminded me of the pastors in the churches who misuse their authority and husbands who abuse their wives emotionally with "gaslighting," a tactic that others in authority use to gain more power over subordinates to make them question their reality and their purpose for existence. This new reporting relationship was all too familiar. But this time a different gaslighting tactic was used: the use of what is near and dear to you as ammunition. They know how important your children are to you, and they know how important your identity is to you on this matter, so they attack the foundation of your being. In this case, it was the choice I had made to care for my daughter and my grandson.

I requested meetings on a number of occasions with my immediate supervisor with a sense of urgency, yet one occurred that made it clear that such conversations were not safe. It was laced with a passive aggressive tone that informed me of this, "Your former boss isn't here now; those days are over!" Eventually, after two previous evaluations that documented deficiencies in the output of my work, some of which were true, there was a common thread. I was not advised about any "lack of performance" during the performance periods. I was only advised during the quarterly evaluation periods and thus, not given the opportunity to improve during a given quarter. In fact, I had been candid with myself and my supervisor on these matters and repeatedly expressed the need to have more personal contact with her as I worked in a silo. I noticed I had not been assigned to manage any RFPs in a while and yet, despite this deviation from my actual job description, I'd expressed my desire to improve the quality of my work with consistency and under the new leadership. But on December 6, 2018, my energy toward this shifted. During a weekly check-in call, I was accused of being "passive aggressive" and "bringing negativity to our team" based on an email I'd sent to other members of our RFP team earlier that week. The email read, "Hi Team, I have not worked with you all in a while on any RFPs, so I am simply touching base. I wish you all happy holidays! Also, while I know we all receive the RFP365 notifications, I wanted to share that I was able to read some of the information at this link [link provided] with the email that was sent below and found it very helpful. So, I am passing it on to you as well. Take care!" Although I asked for one, I was never given an explanation of what was "passive aggressive" and "negative" in this email. I was simply told, "This is an example of how you come across to people and you don't realize it." Given that explanation, I chose to no longer discuss the matter with only my immediate supervisor and her boss who told my immediate boss to give me that feedback, but with her, her boss and HR. Interestingly, when I had wanted to loop in our unit vice president, I was told it was "Not protocol to have him involved." While what felt like bullying and harassment was unacceptable, it was during all the following matters in this situation that I realized HR departments do not work for employees as much as they work for the employer and research shows that employees rarely survive PIPs.

I contemplated filing a discrimination complaint against the company with the EEOC after seeking counsel with a well-known and well-respected HR executive. The statute of limitations gave me six months from the time of the alleged infraction, which was December 6, 2018. But God had a different plan in mind that had little to do with me! It was a clear plan that my God-designed purpose was to enrich others during my lifetime- mainly my children and oftentimes my co-workers. Moreover, my plans, dilemmas, and purpose in life are never solely about me. Yet, He taught me that I could miss this critical lesson by thirteen inches, the distance between my head and my heart. The real purpose of these employment circumstances would lead me to my knees and not to the EEOC and it was evident that my energy and time would be best spent in seeking gainful employment elsewhere. I began my search for a new job shortly after my daughter returned to my home after she'd relocated with my grandson to an Army base in Belgium.

Shortly before the Christmas holiday, I received a call for a job interview in an area where I had wanted to relocate ten years prior, after my divorce. A month later, I accepted an offer. I submitted my resignation letter the day after signing my offer letter on January 16, 2019. My resignation was effective forty-eight hours later, on January 18, 2019 at the close of business. I saw no need to adhere to the standard protocol of giving a two-week notice. I did not have the time. My new position started on February 4, 2019. I knew the respect I had commanded and the professionalism for which I was known amongst my coworkers had not burned any bridges. One month later after I had relocated to my new position, I received a call from my daughter in Belgium. She informed me that she was diagnosed with an auto-immune disease and that she was entitled to a "compassionate transfer" due to this newly discovered medical condition. She was allowed to choose an Army base near me which happened to be located twenty-five miles up the road from my new home! She and my grandson were transferred in June 2019 and lived with me until base housing became available. God had the final say! He orchestrated my relocation to a new state so I could help my family. But He also helped me get the language right in my own thinking and understanding about myself, an invaluable lesson learned on the heels of the 100+ emails I received from coworkers when they heard of my resignation.

Every relationship that involves commitment, whether in a marriage or between an employee and an employer, requires a foundation upon which trust can be built. I was not taught to trust people based on the color of their skin. The level of my trust in others correlates directly with the people that show me that they are trustworthy and not so much on discussions of the topic! Myopic racism unveils the intent often incorporated against others based on their agenda to eliminate people of color who they view as a threat! It infects others, especially those who have only formed an opinion of you based on what they have heard about you. They are the ones who are most susceptible to this mental contagion. Oftentimes, you cannot disinfect the areas to which this infection spreads. It deeply infects the minds of others who are part of an inner corporate world that operates based on a model of a designed membership. This membership seems to think less of dedicated employees than of those who have been hand-picked to advance the corporate agenda. It is the country club within corporate America–an entity whose foundation is "designed exclusion" now trying to save its face with "diversity and inclusion" efforts. But such efforts cannot erase the false narratives and the attempts to assassinate a person's character. Pray for another door to open onto a new platform of performance and never sacrifice your family in doing so, no matter what!

Shut Up and Color

Troii Devereaux

AS A NEW Airman in the United States Air Force, I had experienced blatant racism for the first time by my very first supervisor. I'm originally from Washington, DC and it truly is a melting pot. The schools I've attended consisted of Black children as the majority, but there were children of all ethnicities around me. Diversity wasn't a new concept, and to be honest, a name wasn't placed on it until I'd joined the military. Of course, I've read about racism and we were taught about the Civil Rights movement, highlighting the efforts of Dr. Martin Luther King, Jr, Malcolm X, Medger Evers and Rosa Parks, just to name a few, but as far as my experience goes, it was as if it was a thing of the past.

The year was 1999 and I had recently graduated high school. Once the summer was over, I flew for the very first time in my life to San Antonio, Texas where I would spend six weeks learning how to be an Airman and then another three months to learn the basics of my craft. I was eighteen years old, had virtually no work experience and was just excited for what was to come of a career in the military. My supervisor, who I'll refer to as "Sergeant Sanders," would perform the bare minimum of his duties with regard to shaping and molding me as a new member in my unit. He was responsible for my on-the-job training, reinforcing what

I had learned so that it would be seamless during my transition to my first duty station and establishing expectations while holding me accountable. However, my white female counterpart would receive many opportunities that I would not be afforded during his tenure there.

I had arrived in February of 2000 to Andrews Air Force Base, Maryland, which was literally around the corner to where my family lived. I was excited to be the first person in my generation to join the military, and as corny as it sounds, I was excited to make my family proud. Before meeting Sergeant Sanders, I was greeted by my sponsor "Airman Saxon," which simply put is a person assigned to you to assist with your transition to your new duty station. She was warm and welcoming, assisted me with getting settled into my dorm room and explained how the dining facility operated. We exchanged phone numbers and she let me know that if I had any questions, I could come knock on her door or that I could call her. My first encounter with Sergeant Sanders was a very formal one. He introduced himself as my supervisor, but that he would be leaving soon and that he wouldn't be around very much. I did not recognize his less than enthusiastic attitude about getting to know me as his newest Airman because of how excited I was to get started at my new job. He never smiled, nor did he ever look me in my eyes and I just thought that he was supposed to be that way because he was my supervisor.

Sergeant Sanders quickly explained to me what my duties were and what I couldn't do on the job. He would say things like, "Don't read anything other than the material that has been issued to you while at the front desk. Don't have your friends hanging around when you're supposed to be working." Naturally, as time went on, I began to make friends on and off the job. Even if I was speaking with my coworkers, he would be sure to come over to me and tell me that "We've got a job to do, so all the talking is unnecessary." Again, I thought that he was drilling these things into me because I was new and so that I would remain professional on the job. I didn't read too much into it at the time, but I felt as if I was always doing something wrong, so I just did what I was told. It wasn't until I noticed how "friendly" Sergeant Sanders was to my white female counterpart, that I began to question his motives.

Airman Golf, who I had become friends with during my training in Texas, was the person I shared my bathroom with, in the dormitory. She was bubbly, very sweet, but I noticed that she was always focused on things that she could do to volunteer in the community versus learning the job. Sergeant Sanders was not her supervisor, but ensured that she received mentorship, assigned her duties that were commensurate with someone of a higher rank so that she would be set up for future opportunities and awards based not only on the unfair advantage given, but also off of my contributions at our job. Airman Golf was assigned as an alternate to me and we were in charge of paying contractors and ensuring that the services rendered to the government were evaluated professionally and accurately. I will not lie and say that his attention and mentorship didn't make me a bit salty toward the both of them, but I genuinely liked her, so I ensured that I kept my emotions at bay.

It wasn't until I was placed under another supervisor, Sergeant Posely, who was also white, that I noticed I was being treated differently from my counterparts. She asked questions, especially since my workload was heavier than the others. My responsibility was much bigger, yet Airman Golf and others had been reaping the benefit of being given credit for my work, whether they knew it or not. Once Sergeant Posely started asking questions, she began to enact a more fair and equitable structure in the office that benefitted us all, and not just those that qualified for the "good ole boy" treatment. I learned you didn't even have to be good at what you do to fit in this "club," but I also learned that

I and others that looked like me, weren't welcome. Airman Golf would go on to ask me if I was sad that Sergeant Sanders was leaving because she was. She told me it was nice of him to always look out for her even though he wasn't her direct supervisor. She wasn't aware that he did things for her that he did not do for me. But I can understand why and how she was oblivious to it.

Sergeant Sanders left shortly thereafter, but he wasn't pleased with how Sergeant Posely addressed his supervision tactics with me and let me be aware of it, too. During our last meeting, he'd explained to me that if I wanted to be successful in the Air Force, that I needed to "fall in line" with what I was told and not ask so many questions. I came to the meeting with high hopes because of all of the positive feedback I had been receiving. I had won Airman of the Quarter and had been coined by my commander and a professional group on my base. I just knew he was going to congratulate me on a job well done and let me know how much of a pleasure it was having me as a subordinate. He basically let me know that he was far from impressed with me on the job and otherwise, despite what other higher ups had to say about me. I remember asking him if there was something that I'd done for him to treat me the way that he did. He brushed me off, letting me know that he thought I was being sensitive. He told me that he hadn't done anything to me that wasn't done to him. I then asked him, "Did you like the way you were treated by the supervisor you're referring to?" Sergeant Sanders looked at me for a few seconds before saying anything. It was strange, because he usually gave me the courtesy of addressing me with eye contact. He then replied, "No," and left it at that. We never spoke another word to each other ever again. I will admit, he broke me down during that conversation, but the fire he ignited in me would burn for years to come.

I ensured that I kept up with him and where he was. If he got promoted, I made sure I was the same rank. And then I passed him. He will probably never know how those few months under his direction affected me, but I would always keep him in the back of my mind. I encountered people like him throughout my twenty years in the military, but I made sure to use them as fuel too. Those experiences and individuals would shape me into a person who would strive for promotions and leadership opportunities to later place myself at the table to affect change. Especially for people who looked like me.

I had to master the art of speaking and articulating my thoughts clearly enough to ensure people were comfortable when dealing with me, that I always had to be better and continuously show and prove that I deserved to be there. It was truly exhausting to do these things, but necessary in order to be respected and considered an equal. My career consisted of many more ups than downs, however, I was able to learn from all of my experiences to ensure that I extended that same structure to those that came after me, just as Sergeant Posely had. I will always be grateful to her, because had she not been around when she was, I'm 100% positive that I would have allowed that first experience with racism to cut my military career short.

See How Easy it Ain't

Joanne Meredith

You Can Fire a Company

"THIS ISN'T WORKING so we're going to ask you to leave today." The new director, Bobbi, who had started six weeks ago, was standing behind her desk in a state of rage and fear. The human resource representative, Sara, and I were sitting at the round table across from her desk. I had just returned from lunch and after our morning interaction I was expecting some kind of reaction from Bobbi but not necessarily this one. I could feel my body become warm. The warmth you feel when the world is moving around you and you are standing still. Blood was rushing through my veins at what felt like ninety miles a minute, but I had managed to keep my composure. "I understand," I replied. "Will you at least give me a box to pack my things?" Bobbi threw her hands in the air. The scow on her face and the anger in her voice was a clear indication that she was annoyed by my request and likely just due to my existence. "Sara will get you whatever you need," she hissed.

Truth be told, I did not need much, if even that box. Weeks earlier, I had already taken eight years of my belongings home. My request was a mixture of sarcasm and relief. In a short time, I learned what pushed Bobbi's buttons, and unknowingly managed to press them frequently. I can't say I was surprised by her recent decision. We were oil and water and God was granting my wish.

I was offered and had accepted a new position and resigned just days ago. "You won," Wendy, my colleague said when I had told her I was leaving and wondered why Bobbi was not ecstatic when I submitted my letter. "Won? Won what?" I asked. "It's not what but how. You won because you resigned. She wanted to suck your brain of all your knowledge and expertise and then turn around and fire you." Wendy was probably right. Bobbi had shared with me that she *"knew"* about me and my successful team before she had arrived. She was aware that we had won two prestigious fundraising awards. It was her intention to win an award under her leadership. Bobbi even showed me the spot where she planned to hang the framed announcement. The way Bobbi saw it, I beat her at her own game. Asking me to leave immediately was her way of trumping me … or so she thought.

It was no secret that I had zero respect for her. I made it very clear to leadership before she'd arrived. "You have hired the least qualified candidate," I said to Sharon, the assistant vice president who led the hiring. Sharon knew she needed me. She also knew we did not like one another, and I did not trust her. "You have one or two daughters in college?" she asked. *Really?* Was this woman really trying to use my children to keep me in this job? At that moment, I realized how much I did not truly respect her. She got her job at this university because of who she was and not what she could do.

"Did you select her, too? She doesn't even know best practices," I scolded the consultant. "Joanne, just as Bobbi has to prove to you that she can do the job, you have to prove to her you can do your job." Wow. If the increase in revenue and donors during my tenure didn't prove I could do my job, nothing I did would make that clear.

"I think she's going to do great things," the vice president shared, as he "just happened" to be walking by my office one day.

"Hmm," was all I could muster up. He's rarely in our building and even less on this side of the office. It was clear he was summoned by Sharon to speak with me to get me on board. Sharon was counting on me to be a good sport and train her new protégé.

We had two more experienced applicants. Bobbi was the youngest, the least qualified, had the least amount of experience, and hands down the rudest ... at least to me. As everyone reaffirmed her inexperience, I knew my time had come. Clearly, my opinions, professional contributions, and years of service carried little weight. If they did, only time would tell.

You're Not Good Enough

Bobbi's hiring was the icing on the cake. While Sharon was counting on me to save her and her bad decision, I was planning my exit. The day she came to speak with me to say Bobbi was the candidate that would be hired was the day I began making my plan to leave. She didn't know me, and truth be told she wasn't interested in getting to know me. I'd seen this scenario before early in my career. It was my first professional job right out of college. I was hired as an underwriting manager for a small public television company right outside of Washington, D.C. My supervisor was a white male. No matter what I did, it was not good enough. What I later found out, when I had a new woman supervisor, it was too good. But she wasn't threatened by me. She went to her boss and said, "Joanne can do my job." Her honesty and transparency got me a raise.

When I had a male supervisor, one of my duties was to plan a live television auction. I was responsible for every detail of this event from the auction items to live TV production. I was doing it for three successful years. Until ... Albert, a coworker, decided he wanted to be in charge of the TV auction. Albert was not the brightest person, but all it took was for him to go to our supervisor and it was done. "Joanne, we're going to let Albert coordinate this year's auction." "Why?" I asked. "We think Albert can bring in different items and get us a broader audience," our supervisor said.

I couldn't even process what was being said. I was young and unequipped to handle or counter this insult. So, Albert was given resources to hire three part-time team members who were responsible for securing the items. I sat in the same office as Albert. There was heavy–traffic and activity. It appeared that all was going well for Albert. It looked great from the outside so much so that I began to agree, maybe this was the best decision to have Albert do the TV auction. Maybe they were right. Maybe I wasn't good enough for the job.

Three weeks before the auction, our supervisor summoned me to his office. Up until this time, we passed one another in the hallway or lobby but did not spend time together. So, what could the conversation be about? "Joanne, we need you to help Albert with the TV auction." I was stunned but still angry. "No," I replied. "You gave it to Albert, and he needs to do all of it as I did."

"Joanne, he can't do it! We're three weeks from the auction and no items are logged in the system. We don't know how much or what items we have. The auctioneer hasn't been confirmed. The script for the night hasn't been started so production can't start on the graphics. We need you to help him," my supervisor said. I had not noticed the wrinkle lines across his forehead or how much he appeared to have aged. His thick curly hair was now gray. Clearly, his decision and Albert had taken a toll on him.

I didn't care. I was still insulted and unwilling to help. "You didn't think he could do the job before you gave him *my* TV auction?" I thought you said he could bring in more variety to the auction. And he may have, you just don't know what you have or if you have enough for four hours of live TV."

"I was wrong to take the auction from you. I know that now. Albert asked if he could do it and I made the wrong decision. You should know, this isn't just my request. Randy told me to ask you to step-in. If you don't there won't be an auction this year." Randy was the general manager. He and I both were from Buffalo, New York. That's about all we had in common. I did step-in and it was worse than anyone had thought.

We scrambled to get the final auction items, complete the script, populate the database, secure the volunteers, and auctioneer all just in time for the live broadcast. Albert thanked me profusely for *"helping"* him. Shortly after that, he left to take a university job in Washington, D.C. He was fired not too long after he started.

What Sharon did not know was this episode with Albert was my first SHEIA — my first *See How Easy it Ain't* — experience. SHEIA sustains me, supports me, keeps me focused and prepares me for how to respond to what is happening in the moment. It also reminds me of who I am and what talents and gifts I have been given. SHEIA came to me one evening as I was leaving work. I was frustrated by always having to fight for promotions, opportunities, being included in meetings, and getting recognized for what I'd done for the university.

For years I pushed down what I thought was happening, almost in denial. I was good enough to solve the problems, provide solutions, come to the rescue but not good enough to sit at the decision-making table. This form of exclusion made me question "What's wrong with myself?" But expecting to play along and to be a good sport showed me it was time to fire this university and do what was best for me. Sometimes we have to let go and take our gifts where we will be appreciated and recognized for our contributions. Being recognized is not always about a salary, but about seeing you for who you are, what you contribute and letting them *see 'how easy it ain't.'*

Bobbi failed, miserably. She had lied about her numbers and she left. She went to another university and was there less than a year before they fired her. The university reached out to me after she was gone and offered me a position. I happily declined it.

Why? One: Because it was not at the same level at which they hired Bobbi. Two: Because I am more than good enough, and I deserve better.

Unconscious Bias

....

ADR

THERE IS SO much to say about having an opportunity to work for a world renown household brand name. The esteem, the perks and recognition; even the people I'd met confirmed how lucky I was. Although I was what they called back then a temp, it was still an opportunity of a lifetime. I was convinced that I had enough talent and personality to eventually convert my status from a contractor to a full-time employee. After all, I was smart, experienced, attractive and had a great personality. How could I lose? How could I get this far through the door and then have a seat at the table? I leaned all the way in and performed from day one, that's how. My talent and capabilities would not and could not be denied regardless of the color of my skin, ethnicity, or education.

The team was made up of about twenty talent acquisition professionals that included six coordinators. I was the second to last coordinator to join the team as a contractor. Elsa was the last one to be hired. A quiet, petite woman from an unfamiliar part of Europe. At that time, I was not as well traveled as I am today. Elsa was one of the two Caucasian coordinators on the team. The rest of the coordinators were people of color. I have to admit the diversity on the team, in terms of age, gender and ethnicity was fairly balanced; at least in my opinion. Even though I was a person of color, I didn't look like any of the other people on my team nor did I share the same drive or work ethic. The team was pretty relaxed. The coordinators for the most part, were reserved and naturally submissive. The role was the administrative support to the recruiters so it was quite easy to perform in such a way. I, myself, was much more vocal and proactive. We each supported two, sometimes three recruiters. I had the two best recruiters. We complimented one another's work style and they supported me 100% in everything that I did and vice versa. My thought was that because they were remote, they always had something to prove. That's how I became the talent acquisition extraordinaire.

I solicited new projects to work on to expand my knowledge and build rapport with other, full time recruiters on site. I'd built a relationship with my manager outside of the office. I was truly learning the politics of corporate America in the crash course of "baptized by fire." It was important that people knew me, liked me and respected my work. Truth be told, I loved every minute of it. The people, the lessons, the environment and the awesome food in their amazing food court. Did I forget my paychecks? I failed to mention that I was paid generously. Nothing could go wrong…absolutely nothing.

In an effort to begin tracking my Black girl excellence, a folder in my Lotus Notes was created and named "Kudos." This folder was where I had saved every single compliment received from my team members, my manager and customers. I learned early on from one of my recruiters that everyone you come in contact with is indeed a customer, and that keeping track of your wins was evidence of your stellar performance. That was the key to opening doors, and so I did. By the time the fourth quarter rolled around and headcount opened up, I was locked and loaded with a year of experience in my contractor role. I had a folder full of why I should become a permanent employee.

I was selected as a finalist for the open full time Coordinator position. I was so elated. This was my chance. I remember going to Macy's to get a brand new, navy blue skirt suit just for this interview. I also purchased some pearls and matching earrings. I was going to interview as though I was coming in from the street. Curious, poised, confident and experienced. I received my interview information including who would be on the panel. The interview team included one of the most respected and admired recruiters in the company. He also happened to be a big fan of my work and biggest supporter. I'd spent a year supporting him. He had coached and mentored me, encouraging me to apply for the position. Like I said before, I was super excited, and I knew I had a good chance of being hired full time. I had done the work, built the relationships and put in the time.

On the day of the interview, I learned that my highly respected and recognized recruiter would no longer be participating in the interviews. I remember feeling slightly miffed by this last-minute change. That morning I attempted to make small talk with him and others on the team, but no one seemed to be in the talkative mood. As a matter of fact, there was very little eye contact between him and I. It was as if the energy in the office made a cold shift. Despite the sudden chill in the office, I maintained a positive attitude and walked into the interview with a little extra confidence. Hair in a bun, pearls and navy blue skirt suit that said, "hire me." I impressed myself with my humility, inquisitiveness in the way I'd articulated my experience.

Elsa got the job.

The feedback I'd received was that my interview was impressive and that I was great talent, but the recruiter preferred to work with someone who was familiar with "her work style" and her clients. They added that it had nothing to do with me or my ability to do the job. I sat in my car and played back the entire two weeks prior to the interview up until the day of the interview. I replayed my answers to their questions. I even recalled my success stories shared, recommendations and support from the other recruiters. Why was I not selected based on my ability to do the job? Was that not the purpose of the interview?

I later learned that this particular recruiter had known challenges with other people of color on the team and in fact had not worked with any of them. She preferred to work with people she had worked with in the past or already had relationships with. That seems okay on the surface until I learned the real problem was that she never built relationships with people of color nor did she create the opportunity to work with them. I had interviewed with someone who would never consider my experience or qualifications simply because of the color of my skin. In today's world it is called "unconscious bias." Corporate America continues to create and soften racism that exists and continuously finds ways to soften the blatant disregard and respect for talented people of color.

I remember feeling like the joke was on me. Everyone in the office, including the recruiter who was initially on the interview panel knew that I did not stand a chance in getting that position. I'd felt used. On the day that I learned of the hiring managers hiring preference, all I could feel was resentment and rejection. I could not believe that all of my hard work did not afford me a full-time opportunity. All the late night, hours and working weekends didn't mean anything to the people I thought so highly of and who I'd thought had thought highly of me. Then I started thinking about benefits and holiday pay that I wouldn't get. It hurt me that I didn't get all of those things because of the color of my skin. The feeling of disappointment lasted for a few weeks until I realized that was not going to help. Instead, I continued to do my best work and looked for other opportunities within the company as well as outside the company.

It wasn't long before I got an FTE offer with another company. After all that, I learned that as a woman of color we are always expected to exceed expectations, do more than our Caucasian counterparts but never expect anything in return because no one owes us anything. We owe it to ourselves to do our best so that we can be an example for others. We are here to learn. We come as students. Now whenever I take a contract, I do what I can to the best of my abilities, and I do not apply for a job without asking questions about the manager or the position. I always ask if they already have someone in mind or if the position was created for a specific internal person. I also make it a point not to apply for a position unless someone of influence makes a strong recommendation that I apply. Corporate America is a game with a lot of office politics. If you don't know who the players are, you are guaranteed to get played.

I'll Build My *Own* Table

Danisha D. Allen

WHAT I'VE LEARNED about being racially profiled on a job is that it sucks. I learned that it absolutely hurts deep down in my core because I've been profiled so much because of my name, how I look, how I carry myself, even my education. And I almost let that old nagging voice of imposter syndrome get me a few times. I've sought out mentorship to try to seek advice on how to deal with racism in the workplace. I've tried to seek out mentorship to figure out how to get ahead as a young Black woman with a lot of talent and a lot of skills. And when you say that you have these things, you're often viewed as being very self-centered or egotistical. I'm none of those things, but I'm very confident in what I've worked extremely hard for over the course of twenty years. I found myself being in a lot of boardrooms and corporate spaces with just white people, namely white men. Self-admittedly, many had no prior experiences with other Black people or had never worked with a Black woman. I'd changed the way I dress. I even went so far to shorten and whitewash my name to "Dani" so that I could get past the resume sub-mission process and into actual interviews. I watered down my Southern accent so that I wouldn't have to keep hearing how "uneducated" I sound when I speak. I've made concessions to change a lot of things about myself physically, but the one thing that's remained consistent no matter what I look or sound like is my ability to perform my job and do it well. There were times that I've had few regrets about career moves I've made, good or bad. I've faced many racial dilemmas throughout my career and survived to write about them today. The decision I made to join a small startup at the recommendation of an "ally" is *the one* I will spend years trying to live down and make sense of. Before I knew it, I saw a different side of him at the next job. He'd taken advantage of my diversity status for his personal gain. I was one of the few Black people that he'd ever encountered that thought and performed with intentionality, intelligence, and excellence. He saw a chance to gain favor in the eyes of his new employer by checking two boxes with me: non-white and female.

After starting my new role, I was introduced to a junior analyst I was tasked with training to eventually do my job one day. I got stuck with a "Karen." Her name wasn't Karen, but she behaved like a *Karen*. There was already a lot of pressure on me to learn my new role and do it well, but also mentor someone who was emotionally unstable. I didn't sign up for this nor was it disclosed to me the personality challenges she was experiencing. Instead, I was told she'd been with the company for about eight years before my arrival and was intimately knowledgeable of the products, how they worked and were designed. I tried to tread lightly because I needed her for information purposes. She was one of the few who managed to provide me with a bit of history of how the company started and grew. At first, I was all for empowering women since we're often overlooked for opportunities of advancement in the workplace. Yes, she was white, but that was nothing new to me, so I tried to connect with her on a personal level. We were both mothers of kids born on the same date, we were close in age, and we shared many laughs over the silly things our husbands did. I

166

thought this was a relationship I could grow to appreciate while I was there. At least until I got to see "Karen" in action.

"Karen" was constantly emotional, always crying, always having fits and storming out of meetings. A lot of days, I didn't know if something was really wrong with her. And if I had behaved that way, as a Black woman, I would be escorted out of the job and be asked to never come back again. If you've ever had the pleasure of spending significant time with a toddler, you'd see how quickly their moods can swing from one end of the pendulum to the next and be accompanied by crying and whining. This was Karen. She had crying fits that would rival my two-year old's. I guess I wasn't sure why she was allowed to remain other than the fact that she had eight years of tenure and her tears were precious. Ah, those precious white woman tears. They were more precious than gold. She had mastered weaponizing them and knew they could get her into any room and get a "yes" from anyone no matter what she did. On the other hand, I wasn't allowed to let someone know how uncomfortable her excessive display of discontentment was making me and how it was complicating any opportunity I had to mentor her. Rather than HR listening and taking action, I was instead told I could decide to go elsewhere. At that point, I had started looking but only received lowballed offers. I was backed into a corner. I could stay and endure being constantly questioned about being Black, which I found very odd, or I could take a huge pay cut and start over. I opted to stay since I now had a child to care for as a sign of "strength." I tried to stick to my guns for a lot of days, I found myself either running to the car at the end of the day, crying on the way home, or just seething mad about some asinine conversation I'd had just hours before. I was determined not to let them see me sweat. They would not get the best of me.

Fast forward a few months into the job and "Karen" asks me to go out to lunch. I told her I didn't mind going and I'd even drive.

She followed me out to my car then started laughing. At that time, I drove a Buick Enclave, a fact that didn't get past "Karen's" complaining ass. As she buckled her seatbelt, she made it a point to say nonchalantly that she'd never known anyone young that drove a Buick. For me, that was nothing foreign. I grew up in the south–everyone had a damn Buick. I turned the ignition so I could quickly get the air conditioning blowing and move out the hot stale air in the car. Before I got out of the car that morning, I forgot to turn down my radio, so whatever song was playing on the radio at the time was just getting started. I began to sing along, and she then proceeded to ask if the song playing was "gangster rap," (Insert eye roll.) First of all, it's 2016 and no one calls hip-hop "gangster rap." Secondly, if she thought the R&B group Jagged Edge was "gangster" or "rapping" in any way, then she would've died listening to NWA. I looked at her dead in her eyes and said "Sweetheart, this is the furthest thing from rap music. This is called R&B. And they're *singing* a song." While looking at her, I asked if she'd ever even heard a rap song. At that point, I didn't listen for a response. Anything else said would have been a complete and utter bullshit response. I proceeded to turn my radio up louder and sang at the top of my lungs while we drove off to Panera Bread to get salad. "Karen" never rode with me again.

The encounters with "Karen" didn't get any better, but I tried to persevere and work through them by taking all of her micro-aggressions in stride. A few times the entire team went out to lunch. Most days I wanted to be left alone, but I'd be asked to come. Of course, everybody was always excited for me to go because I was the "Cool Black girl," the token of the group. And everybody wanted to ask me all the questions they were dying to know about being Black in a safe space. What made them think talking to me was "safe?" Maybe it's because I never gave the impression that I would be extremely judgmental or cared about the types of questions asked. But deep down inside, they bothered me. They bothered me because these people, my coworkers, had never taken the chance or mustered up the audacity to get to know someone outside of their immediate circles that involved or included someone like me. Most of these outings included me being forced to listen to how she'd never known anyone Black in her life. I know I'd be curious about a lot if I were her. However, curiosity is a world away from being a walking stereotype or monolith. On multiple occasions I was asked about my hair, about my clothes, what it was like growing up in the south, and even how to properly cook and season collard greens. It seemed that never working with Black people was really a thing.

A new junior, hot-shot developer was hired. One day, we had all gone out to lunch again and the subject of race once again made its way into the discussion. He admitted that he'd never worked with another Black person, period, male or female. I was then asked, "How do you do that?" Okay...I'm looking like a deer in headlights. I've heard some things in my day, but I wasn't ready for that one. At all. So, I ask, "What do you mean exactly?" My response was something I took my time with, mulled over, tasted with all of its question's ignorance and filth; something I'd almost responded to with disdain and a fully healthy read. I opted out. Instead, I said "You know, the same way you would work with a white person—you just do your job and you are respectful." I can't comprehend why people say such things after forty plus years post-segregation. How dare he ask me something so insulting and disrespectful. I am Black, but I am not representative of the entire race of the entire culture. We are so intricately beautiful and complex in so many ways. There's no way that my life's existence could account for the millions and billions of stories that our people have lived through and endured since mankind was formed. Respect my people.

Another time, at this same job with the same group of people,

I went to a happy hour gathering against my better judgement. I knew better. Damn, did I know better. Again, I thought I was being nice by trying to look past their perceived judgment and ignorance, willful or not. I went along with it. While we waited for our orders to come out, we were having a conversation about TV shows. As far as I can recall, most of everything up to that point was sort of cordial. But when you're having a conversation with people who can't go ten solid minutes without putting their foot in their mouths, things are bound to take a turn for the worst. It didn't take long. I was asked a few questions about Black TV shows and Black TV characters. Red flags went up–again. And then it happened–the last nerve I had reserved for them was torched to a crisp.

Mr. hot-shot Developer looks me in my face while laughing and says "Hey, well, how come *you're* not rolling *your* neck and snapping your fingers like all the other Black girls we see on TV?" Honey, if you could have seen the look on my face, if you've never seen a dark chocolate Black woman become red (and I am chocolate), you've never seen someone be pissed. For the life of me I couldn't understand how someone could insult my humanity as a real living and breathing being and my proud HBCU education by asking me to soft-shoe for them by further perpetuating a stereotype that they had only seen on TV. How dare you? A lot of times we reduce ourselves and put on a show and entertain the masses. I am not a fictional character. My experiences will not be reduced to being things of the sort.

I'm so tired of having people ask if they can touch my hair. Or if my current hair is designed using only my real hair? Or how long it takes to do my braids and if braids are really called extensions. Or how they're installed. All the while, their faces read "I wish I had hair like yours. My hair is just really flat. It has no body. It has no shape." I'm over it. Oh my gosh–go get a wig already. That's why they're made. If you are envious of my hips,

170

my hair, my lips, or my breasts, go buy yourself some. If you're bored with how you look, go spice up your own life, but don't use me to be this person you live vicariously through. I'm over it in professional settings. Thank goodness for the Crown Act.

The best advice ever given to me was to continue to push forward no matter what it looks like and what it feels like. Corporate America has really inspired me to fight for change, not just in a feminist aspect, but specifically for Black women. In the world of IT (information technology), there are very few faces that look like mine and I've encountered even less in almost 20 years. So many of our stories often go untold and the challenges that we face day-to-day often go unchecked. A lot of times we're told "Hey, just go talk to HR." The truth of the matter is your HR department exists to protect the interests of the business from a human standpoint and not the humans it employs. Women like me often find themselves not receiving any traction or any help from the higher-ups. To overcome it all, I've learned that I can only look to myself or rally and gather with the few other women I've encountered that look like me and have shared similar experiences. Before this year, I only had three other Black women I could call to shed my feelings and frustrations and share my triumphs with who would really understand. Today, thanks to Niani Tolbert and her #HIREBLACK Initiative, I've been able to cheer on, support, and mentor hundreds of thousands of women who have taken up the cause behind her vision to change the narrative for us as we forge ahead.

In the real world, the only consideration Black women are being given in these diversity conversations is how to use our natural maternal skills to fill these powerless, figurehead roles. We are not your mama at work. I am not your corporate mother. Too often, when there's a problem with race or injustice in this world, we are always on the front lines trying to fix things. I'm tired of Black women being responsible for the outcomes of making sure people who are Black, brown, LGBTQIA, or of any intersection-ality of the like are included. We didn't create racism. So why are we often tasked with the responsibility of fixing it? We're not the ones who are discriminating. We're being discriminated against. Likewise, if having a DE&I role is causing great concern, then it's obvious that diversity training is just as trashy if not worse. Based on my personal experience, I feel that everything we've been taught about diversity and inclusion in the workplace is absolutely wrong. Who's writing these manuals? Who's coming up with these ideas about how to handle situations where the people involved are often white on one side and Black on the other? My life doesn't have time to wait for a politically correct delivery of a critical message. My life depends on meaningful action today.

And for that, I know diversity, equity, and inclusion (DE&I) training in corporate America is often something made the subject of sick and twisted backroom conversations. I find myself upset, almost shaking with anger and disgust, especially here in 2020, with the fact that it's taken yet another Black man, George Floyd dying at the hands of police, for some corporations to really pour some thought into the necessity of D&I and DE&I roles. These positions sit directly outside of the C-suite of corporations. A lot of times D&I hires are never really given any authority. They hardly ever receive a budget. They normally don't have a single direct report. And after about five years, the people taking these roles often leave because they feel unempowered. And if these D&I and DE&I roles are deemed either powerless or inefficient, the hires that had them are blamed. This then makes it easy for a company to say there was never a diversity problem to begin with. They will say, "See, there was never a problem. We gave you an opportunity to step up and fix it and you couldn't even figure it out." I've seen it with my own two eyes: D&I is simply just a notion, just a set of motions companies go through just to say,

"Hey, we're compliant. We're ahead of the curve. Look at us. We're trending." Excuse me, but Black is not trending. Black is not hip. Black is not a thing to aspire to. It is who *we* are. It is who we've always been. And that's who we will be going forward. If companies want to really promote inclusion, they have to start with getting rid of the white, male dominated culture they've woven into the very fabric of their company's ideology. We have to stop giving them an out. We, Black women, have to stop taking these jobs for the pay and resume boost without holding the companies we represent responsible for ensuring we have all the tools, money, and manpower to invoke lasting effective change.

Racism and sexism in corporate America in fact is a major issue. I've come to that conclusion because I've lived it. Right now, in 2020, less than 2% of current CEOs sitting in the boardroom are Black and even fewer are women. So that means the less than 1% of CEOs of all corporations in America are Black women. I am a Black woman in the world of information technology, and I have yet to see a black woman Chief Technology Officer lead an organization. I know that being an intelligent, confident, direct, and driven Black woman is viewed as a problem everywhere we go. Anytime a Black woman asserts her authority. She's considered angry or aggressive or mad or nasty. I reference how Kamala Harris is being treated right now in the midst of our 2020 presidential election. At the end of the day, it has to end. Black women are often groped and suffer comments about our breasts, about our hips, about the very things that others fantasize about. When these actions make us uncomfortable, we speak up about it and report it. Those reports simply get filed and nothing is done. The onus of being a victim of a sexual attack is often placed back on us as if we've asked to be sexualized or objectified or disrespected. Look at the #metoo movement. The movement was started by a Black woman as a way for us to tell our stories of sexual abuse and seek retribution. By the end of its fanfare, the empathy we should have received was only reserved for white women and their struggles. Because our movement was taken over and represented by the faces of white women, our narratives and our stories were put on the back burner. It seems we won't ever see the day where our safety and security can be fairly addressed in the workplace.

Not surprisingly, there's been little corporate outcry for Brianna Taylor, a Black female EMT from Louisville, Kentucky murdered in her sleep in the middle of the night, outside of women-dominated organizations such as the WNBA. Her death has been in vain thus far because even in her death, considering it happened back in March and it's almost September, still justice has not been served. There has been absolutely no closure for her family, no closure for her friends or the people that fight and push to see her killers be arrested and tried. There's no closure for the countless other Black women who have had to endure mistreatment or lost their lives to police brutality before her—Sandra Bland, Atatiana Jefferson, Pamela Turner, Korryn Gaines, Yvette Smith, and so many others. I will say their names. I could be them. And they *are* me. Let's have an honest moment, if you will. Corporations want to be on the right side of history. Not a single major business in the United States wants to be the one who still pushes hidden racist agendas. None of them will admit that in the year of 2020, the year of our Lord, that more Black people are being murdered by the police and they've done nothing about it. They don't want to say, "Hey, we employ all these Black people, these athletes, these movie stars, but we only care about their skills. We don't care about their lives outside of our sets and outside of our buildings and off of our fields." I think corporations are starting to understand and recognize the power of the Black dollar from a consumer perspective and how much they stand to lose. The Montgomery Bus Boycott of 1955 and 1956 was monumental in the way it allowed Black people to show businesses that they needed us more than we needed them and that we were worth more than just the dollars we spent. But for those of us who are able to work in those businesses, the C-suite still fails to understand the potential implications of not finally seeing us and recognizing us from a corporate perspective. And if they cannot see our Blackness, they will surely miss our femininity.

As a result, last year I had stepped out and I've been blessed to start my own business. I've been able to take all the experiences of the last twenty years and launch it into career coaching for other Black women in the IT world and even helping other Black women who are seeking to pivot and come into the IT sector from other industries. I also help Black people who own small and midsize businesses to develop applications and solutions that make it easier to serve their customers. I love working with Black creatives in the technology space and finding ways to help them retain the intellectual property rights to their ideas and products. My company is doing big things. We're going to make sure women that look like me, that sound like me, that are made just like me, are able to be given credit for the thoughts that they have and own and see them come to fruition. No longer will we sell our dreams short. No longer will we give them away for free because we're here. We're unapologetically Black and we're a bunch of badass women here to build our own tables in corporate America. You can keep your table. We've got our own.

A Word From The Experts

"I Can't Breathe!"
....

Lacrecia Dangerfield, EdD, LPC-MHSP

"I CAN'T BREATHE!" These three words placed together have become the slogan of the Black Lives Matter movement after the murder of Eric Garner. These same three words can be heard spoken by many Black women behind the closed doors of their corporate offices or during the middle of the night when she wakes from a nightmare or is preparing to get out of her car at work. No, they are not having their life strangled out of them by a cop, but the weight and pressure of racist tactics in work-places can have the same traumatic effects as being wrestled to the ground with a knee on your neck taking your life. Women of color experience mental health symptoms and disorders such as anxiety, depression, or post-traumatic stress disorder (PTSD) at an alarming rate.

Anxiety and depression are considered the most commonly diagnosed mental health disorders among women. Some research shows that Black women experience anxiety and depression more intensely and in a chronic manner than their white counterparts (Neal-Barnett, 2018; Watson & Hunter, 2015). The manifestation of these disorders may be expressed differently in Black women more as physical health issues such as high blood pressure, high cholesterol, digestive issues, etc. It is reported that black women will go to their primary care physician due to the physical manifestations of trauma before acknowledging that they have been triggered by a traumatic event and seek out help for their mental health.

As a Licensed Professional Counselor, I utilize the Diagnostic and Statistical Manual of Mental Disorders (DSM-IV) as a standard to diagnose clients who are presented with certain symptoms and behaviors. In my work with high achieving women of color, I have found that most do not meet the classic criteria for generalized anxiety disorder, major depressive disorder, persistent depressive disorder, post-traumatic stress disorders, etc. as defined. However, in my research to find a title for what I see, I've found the terms "high functioning anxiety" and "high functioning depression" to more accurately describe the experiences of these high achieving women of color who have experienced racial and gender related events in their workplace.

What does anxiety and depression look like in high achievers?

High functioning anxiety is in reference to individuals who live with anxiety but function well in different areas of their daily life. These individuals are usually considered high achieving and successful on the outside but inside they are living with constant nervous energy, fear of failure, imposter syndrome, perfectionism, inconsistent sleeping habits, low self-esteem and confidence. Women who experience high functioning anxiety may talk themselves out of seeking help because who will do the work when they are not there, or the perception of losing their position of influence. The continual pressures of institutional racism perpetuate the feeling of anxiety and depression.

High functioning depression can be a companion to anxiety or a separate placeholder in the life of high achieving Black women. This form of depression is more like a low-grade fever, it is persistent without causing debilitating actions. The defining symptoms include overeating or decreased appetite, sleeping too much or bouts of insomnia, lack of energy, low self-esteem, a persistent feeling of sadness or hopelessness, difficulty in concentrating and making decisions and feeling irritable or frustrated. Procrastination, perceived laziness, feeling like an imposter, etc. are other behaviors that women have to combat while functioning at their best. Co-workers, family and friends may not notice that she is suffering in silence because on a good day she is performing as normal. It is not until the bottom falls out that others will notice and wonder what happened. The coupling of anxiety and depression plus the blatant racism or the subtle digs can be the undoing of the high achieving women of color.

What can the high achieving woman do to care for her mental health?

Find a safe and confidential space to talk with a licensed mental health professional.

Here are some options:

- www.therapyforblackgirls.com–an online space for Black women and girls that offers a directory of therapists of color who specialize in a variety of treatment modalities and areas of issues.
- www.openpathcollective.com–a non-profit network of therapists who provide virtual and in-office therapy at a reduced rate for those who are uninsured or underinsured.
- www.betterhelp.com–an online platform that offers counseling sessions via telephone, video and text options for a monthly fee.
- www.psychologytoday.com–provides a directory of therapists, psychologists, and counselors along with other informational resources.

Practice mindfulness

Mindfulness techniques include deep breathing, prayer, meditation, and grounding techniques. An example of a grounding technique is to bring yourself to the present by focusing on your five senses. Name five things you can see, four things you can hear, three things you can feel or touch, two things you can smell and one thing you can taste.

Purposefully plan a mental health day

Mental health days from work are set to reduce stress and to help prevent burnout. When you take a mental health day from work make sure that you unplug from work. You should not be checking your voicemails or emails. It is a day to do nothing but restore and refresh yourself.

Make self-care a daily practice.

Self-care is not selfish. Self-care is deeper than scheduling a manicure/pedicure or a massage. Self-care means to plug into who you are and practice daily things that help you to become a better you. This can include practicing mindful eating, daily prayer and devotion, physical activity, gratitude journaling, drinking water, getting enough sleep, etc.

Remember your mental health is your wealth and well-being!

Lacrecia Dangerfield, EdD, LPC-MHSP is the CEO of Reimprint Your Life Coaching and Counseling in Nashville, TN. Dr. Dangerfield specializes in working with mental health professionals and leaders of color. Her experience includes working over fifteen years in corporate America. She has been in the mental health industry since 2003.

Conclusion

....

WHERE DO WE go from here? Will we ever see a change in corporate America when it comes to the treatment of Black women? I wish I could scream, "Hell yea!" But the grim reality is a resounding, "Hell no." I only see the continued struggle for equity and equality in corporate America when it comes to Black women if we continue to play by their rules. Let's stop pretending that white women are our allies. If they truly were advocating on our behalf we wouldn't be having this conversation. Becky pats us on the back, while negating our experiences behind closed doors. She blatantly tells us that we can't be subjective and that it is wrong for us to talk about our disrespect and not include the disrespect of Asian, Latino and Native American women too. Karen is undermining our efforts, so she and her man can continue to outpace us in pay and widen the wealth gap that has existed for centuries, while moving us further and further away from the so-called American dream. We have to refuse to allow them to rewrite our history and whitewash our stories and start calling a spade a spade. We need to realize that no one is coming to save us and that we have to become our own allies, instead of trying to tear each other down for that one seat in the boardroom.

They won't let us have anything, so we have to stand our ground and take it. Stop asking for respect and start living like we already have it. Stop feeling guilty when we speak out and instead speak louder and bolder. The sooner we understand that we don't have to continue to ask anyone for anything, the better off we will be. We are smart enough to actually go out and create opportunities for ourselves and for other Black women too.

If Black women want a seat at the table they will have to realize that it's no longer about bringing a folding chair as Shirley Chisholm suggested, but saying "fuck their table," and build our own! We have to stop shrinking because we don't fit into a corporate society that wasn't built for us, and begin to understand the impact of building our own. Until we begin to walk in our truths as these twenty ladies did in this anthology, we will continue to be ignored and work in unbearable, slave-like conditions.

The way Black women can begin to shut down racism in corporate America is through economic impact. We have to stop being afraid of numbers and money and understand the value we bring to the capitalistic system that America utilizes us for and figure out how to carve out our own space and build our own wealth, instead of waiting for a handout that is never going to come. We have to learn how to build Black, hire Black, and buy Black, creating the same cycle that has sustained the American system since the founding of this country. We have to see that our dollars are valuable and if we begin to keep them in our own communities, people–white people, will have no choice but to stop and listen to us.

But until we begin to value ourselves and come to grips that it is going to take more than prayer and Jesus to deliver us from systemic racism and stop waiting for an invitation to sit at their table, we will continue to perpetuate this vicious cycle of disrespect over and over again. Use the experiences of the contributing authors to fuel your fire. Allow their stories to give you strength and courage to continue to push forward. And maybe one day our daughters and granddaughters will be the ones who truly shut'em all the way down!

Dr. Carey Yazeed

Made in the USA
Coppell, TX
02 April 2022

75908676R00114